THE LAW OF BUYING AND SELLING

Second Edition

by
Margaret C. Jasper

Oceana's Legal Almanac Series:
Law for the Layperson

2002
Oceana Publications, Inc.
Dobbs Ferry, New York

Library of Congress Control Number: 2002101870

ISBN: 0-379-11366-X

Oceana's Legal Almanac Series: Law for the Layperson
ISSN 1075-7376

To My Husband Chris

Your love and support
are my motivation and inspiration

-and-

In memory of my son, Jimmy

Table of Contents

CHAPTER 6:
WARRANTIES

CHAPTER 7:
UNFAIR AND DECEPTIVE ACTS AND PRACTICES—LIABILITY BETWEEN CONSUMERS AND SELLERS OF GOODS AND SERVICES

CHAPTER 8:
UNFAIR AND DECEPTIVE ACTS AND PRACTICES—LIABILITY AMONG SELLERS OF GOODS AND SERVICES

CHAPTER 9:
TRUTH IN LENDING

CHAPTER 10:
FAIR CREDIT REPORTING

CHAPTER 11:
THE FAIR DEBT COLLECTION PRACTICES ACT

CHAPTER 12:
THE MAIL OR TELEPHONE ORDER MERCHANDISE RULE

CHAPTER 13:
THE TELEMARKETING SALES RULE

CHAPTER 14:
BUYING AND SELLING ON THE INTERNET

ABOUT THE AUTHOR

MARGARET C. JASPER is an attorney engaged in the general practice of law in South Salem, New York, concentrating in the areas of personal injury and entertainment law. Ms. Jasper holds a Juris Doctor degree from Pace University School of Law, White Plains, New York, is a member of the New York and Connecticut bars, and is certified to practice before the United States District Courts for the Southern and Eastern Districts of New York, the United States Court of Appeals for the Second Circuit, and the United States Supreme Court.

Ms. Jasper has been appointed to the panel of arbitrators of the American Arbitration Association and the law guardian panel for the Family Court of the State of New York, is a member of the Association of Trial Lawyers of America, and is a New York State licensed real estate broker and member of the Westchester County Board of Realtors, operating as Jasper Real Estate, in South Salem, New York. Margaret Jasper maintains a website at http://members.aol.com/JasperLaw.

Ms. Jasper is the author and general editor of the following legal almanacs: Juvenile Justice and Children's Law; Marriage and Divorce; Estate Planning; The Law of Contracts; The Law of Dispute Resolution; Law for the Small Business Owner; The Law of Personal Injury; Real Estate Law for the Homeowner and Broker; Everyday Legal Forms; Dictionary of Selected Legal Terms; The Law of Medical Malpractice; The Law of Product Liability; The Law of No-Fault Insurance; The Law of Immigration; The Law of Libel and Slander; The Law of Buying and Selling; Elder Law; The Right to Die; AIDS Law; OThe Law of Obscenity and Pornography; The Law of Child Custody; The Law of Debt Collection; Consumer Rights Law; Bankruptcy Law for the Individual Debtor; Victim's Rights Law; Animal Rights Law; Workers' Compensation Law; Employee Rights in the Workplace; Probate Law; Environmental Law; Labor Law; The Americans with Disabilities Act; The Law of Capital Punishment; Education Law; The Law of Violence Against Women; Landlord-Tenant Law; Insurance Law; Religion and the Law; Commercial Law; Motor Vehicle Law; Social Security Law; The Law of Drunk Driving; The Law of Speech and the First Amendment; Employment Discrimination Under Title VII; Hospital Liability Law; Home Mortgage Law Primer; Copyright Law; Patent Law; Trademark Law; Special Education Law; The Law of Attachment and Garnishment; Banks and their Customers; and Credit Cards and the Law.

INTRODUCTION

This legal almanac explores the law of buying and selling. This area of law includes a wide range of complex consumer-related topics. Thus, a comprehensive study cannot be accomplished in the context of this almanac. Therefore, the author has attempted to provide information which will give the reader a general understanding of the basic law and its application to the consumer.

This almanac sets forth a general discussion concerning the buying and selling of goods and services, basic contractual concepts and governing provisions of the Uniform Commercial Code, and the rights and responsibilities between the buyer and seller/creditor in consumer transactions and finance. This almanac also explores the subject of internet buying and selling, internet auctions, electronic payments, the international on-line marketplace, and privacy issues relating to on-line shopping.

The law applicable to unfair and deceptive acts and practices as it pertains to transactions between a consumer and a seller of goods and services, and to acceptable conduct among sellers of goods and services, is also discussed. The relevant sections of the Uniform Commercial Code are examined, as well as applicable sections of the Restatement Second of the Law of Contracts and the Restatement Third of the Law of Unfair Practices.

The Appendix provides sample documents, applicable statutes, and other pertinent information and data. The Glossary contains definitions of many of the terms used throughout the almanac.

CHAPTER 1:
THE SALE OF GOODS

BASIC CONTRACT LAW

Contract law is primarily derived from judicial decisions, known as the common law, and from statutory law, such as the Uniform Commercial Code. Secondary authority supporting the evolution of contract law comes from sources which influence judicial decision making, such as restatements of the law, treatises, and law reviews.

Applicable sections of the Restatement Second of the Law of Contracts is set forth at Appendix 1.

A contract is an agreement between two or more persons which creates an obligation to do, or refrain from doing, a particular thing. In order to form a valid contract, there must be (1) an offer; (2) acceptance of the offer; (3) consideration; and (4) a mutual agreement by the parties as to the subject matter of the contract, i.e. a "meeting of the minds."

As applied to a consumer transaction, the seller offers to provide the consumer goods or services at a stated price—the consideration. The consumer accepts the offer by paying the mutually agreed upon price.

THE UNIFORM COMMERCIAL CODE

The Uniform Commercial Code (UCC) refers to the set of laws governing commercial transactions which was drafted by the National Conference of Commissioners on Uniform State Laws. The UCC has not been enacted as federal law, however, it is the governing law in the District of Columbia.

The purpose underlying the drafting of the UCC was to promote certainty and predictability of commercial law and, thus, reduce the number of legal disputes arising out of commercial matters.

It was recognized that it would be particularly advantageous if the UCC were uniformly adopted by all of the states with little or no revision or amendment. However, all of the states have adopted some form of the UCC, along with numerous jurisdictional amendments. Thus, uniformity as it relates to the laws of the various states is somewhat of a misnomer, except in the areas of consumer transactions where a federal statute preempts conflicting state law.

The UCC does not claim to be a comprehensive set of commercial laws. For example, there are certain purportedly commercial matters which are not addressed by the UCC, such as the sale of real property, insurance contracts, bankruptcy matters, and suretyship transactions. Such matters are left to the jurisdiction of general contract law.

In addition, certain topics which are covered by the UCC must still rely on non-UCC law for support, guidance and clarification. In addition, where there is a federal law which conflicts with a UCC provision, the federal law will prevail over the UCC.

This almanac is primarily concerned with Article 2 of the UCC which governs the sale of goods. As defined in UCC Section 2-106(1), a sale is the passing of title from the seller to the buyer for a price. Goods means all things which are movable at the time of identification to the contract of sale, i.e. tangible personal property. Throughout this almanac, various citations to applicable sections of the UCC are stated for the reader's information.

CONTRACT FORMATION

General contract law as set forth in the Restatement Second of the Law of Contracts will apply unless it conflicts with a governing UCC provision. The basic contract formation requirements according to general contract law principles, and as superseded by specific provisions of the UCC related to the sale of goods, are set forth below.

The Offer

The Offer According to General Contract Law Principles

Common law contract law generally defines an offer as a proposal to do something which is usually accompanied by an expected acceptance, a counter-offer, or a return promise or act. The offer permits the offeree—in this case, the consumer—the power to accept the offer thus making the offeror's promise a contractual obligation.

As set forth below, there are three basic requirements of a valid offer.

1. Commitment

There must be clear commitment, or intention, by the offeror, to make the offer.

2. Communication

There must be communication of the offer by the offeror to the identified offeree, and the offeree must have actual knowledge of the offer in order to accept it. An exception to the communication requirement exists in the context of a public offer. Obviously, there cannot be identification of the offeree until someone (a) knows that the offer exists and (b) performs the requested act.

3. Definite Terms

An offer must contain definite and certain terms. It is no longer necessary that an offer define all material terms in order to be valid. However, the offer must at least define, with certainty, the subject matter of the contract, so as to show that the parties had a "meeting of the minds" on the most basic aspect of the contract. The court may furnish all other material terms of a disputed contract with reasonable terms.

The Offer Under the Uniform Commercial Code

In order to be a valid offer, a contract governed by the UCC, except in certain cases, need only provide the quantity of items to be sold. Section 2-306(1) of the UCC sets forth an exception to the rule requiring the contract to recite the quantity of items to be sold.

Such an exception exists when a contract for the sale of goods calls for Buyer's purchase of the "total output" of the Seller (an "output" contract), or when the contract calls for Buyer's promise to purchase all the product that Buyer "requires" from the Seller (a "requirements" contract).

In that case, a "reasonable" quantity will be implied by the court should there be a dispute. If there has been a stated estimate, the Court may use this as a guideline to determine a good faith quantity. If there is no stated estimate, the Court may consider the terms of prior output contracts between the parties.

A merchant's firm offer is defined in Section 2-205 of the UCC as an offer by a merchant to buy or sell goods in a signed writing which, by its terms, gives assurance that it will be held open. For example, Merchant makes the following offer to Buyer: "I am offering apples at $10 per bushel. I will hold this offer open for 60 days from the date of this notice. Signed, Merchant."

This is a merchant's firm offer because it is a signed writing which states that the offer will be held open. If the offer had simply stated "I am offering apples at $10 per bushel. Signed, Merchant." This would not constitute a "firm offer" because it does not contain any assurance that the offer would be held open.

If the assurance is supplied by the offeree, the writing must also be signed by the offeror in order to make it a binding firm offer. For example, Merchant states: "I am offering apples at $10 per bushel. Signed, Merchant." Buyer responds: "I received your firm offer for the sale of apples at $10 per bushel, and confirm that we may accept at any time within the next 30 days. Signed, Buyer."

Merchant's offer was not a firm offer because it contained no assurance that the offer would be held open. Since Buyer's writing contained the assurance, in order to be enforceable against Merchant as a firm offer, Merchant must sign Buyer's writing acknowledging the assurance.

The merchant's firm offer is not revocable during the time stated in the writing. However, if there is no time stated in the writing, the offer will be deemed irrevocable for a reasonable period of time. In either case, despite what the writing may state, the period of irrevocability may not exceed three months.

For example, Merchant states: "I am offering apples at $10 per bushel. I will hold this offer open for 3 months from the date of this notice. Signed, Merchant." This offer is thus irrevocable for 3 months. Nevertheless, if the Merchant had stated that the offer would be open for 120 days, the period of irrevocability would still be limited to 3 months according to the statute.

Unlike an option contract, which requires that the offeree give some consideration to hold an offer open for a stated period of time, the merchant's firm offer under the UCC does not require any consideration.

Counter-Offers

A counter-offer is defined as an offer made by an offeree to an offeror relating to the same subject matter as the original offer, and proposing a substituted bargain differing from that proposed by the original offer.

The method of making counter-offers differs depending on whether or not the contract is governed by the UCC.

Counter-Offers in Non-UCC Contracts

The acceptance of an offer must mirror the offer or it will be deemed a counter-offer. If the acceptance adds anything new or different to the original offer, a counter-offer is created which requires an acceptance by the original offeror.

Counter-Offers Governed by the Uniform Commercial Code

The UCC sets forth various rules concerning counter-offers in connection with the sale of goods. Under the UCC, counter-offers are limited to the following two methods:

1. By shipping non-conforming goods as an accommodation, as set forth above; or

2. By making words of acceptance expressly conditioned on a new or different term.

Where the parties to a contract seek to modify the terms of the original contract, the modification would still be enforceable, even without consideration, as long as it was done in good faith, and new duties arise under the contract as a result.

Terminating an Offer

In general, an offer is freely terminable prior to acceptance, and is accomplished by (1) revocation; (2) rejection; or (3) operation of law, as set forth below.

1. Termination by Revocation—Prior to acceptance, an offeror can revoke an offer either (a) expressly or (b) by conduct.

(a) Express Revocation—Express revocation is effective when the offeree receives it. Actual knowledge by the offeree of the offeror's revocation of the offer is not required. It is effective upon receipt whether or not the offeree has yet read it.

(b) Revocation by Conduct—An offer can be revoked by conduct if the offeror does something that would prevent performance of the contract and the offeree gains knowledge of that fact from a reliable source.

2. Termination by Rejection—Prior to acceptance, an offeree can reject an offer either (a) expressly or (b) by conduct.

(a) Express Rejection—Express rejection occurs when the offeree refuses the offer or when the offeree communicates a counter-offer. An express rejection is effective when the offeror has received it. As with express revocation, actual knowledge by the offeror of the offeree's rejection of the offer is not required. It is effective upon receipt whether or not the offeror has read it.

(b) Rejection by Conduct—Rejection by conduct occurs when the offeree lets the offer lapse. For example, if the offeror states that the offer is open for 7 days and the offeree makes no effort to accept the offer within that 7 day period, the offer is deemed rejected by conduct. If the offer does not provide a time period within which it must be accepted, it will be deemed open for a reasonable period of time.

Once an offer has been rejected, it can never be revived, even if the offeree subsequently attempts to accept the offer. In that case, the offeree would be deemed to have made a new offer and would thus be acting as the offeror. Such is the case with a counter-offer as set forth above.

3. Termination by Operation of Law—An offer may be terminated by operation of law in the following three ways:

(a) Intervening Event—Something occurs before acceptance has taken place which makes it impossible to follow through with the offer.

(b) Supervening Illegality—The offer will be terminated if a law is passed which prevents the contract from being performed.

(c) Death or Incapacity—The death or incapacity of either the offeror or offeree will terminate the offer.

Irrevocable Offers

There are certain offers which cannot be terminated and thus deemed irrevocable, as follows:

1. Merchant's Firm Offer—In many states, in connection with the sale of goods, if a merchant puts an offer in writing stating that it will be held open, that offer is irrevocable for the time stated in the writing, or for a reasonable amount of time if the writing is silent as to the time period. A reasonable amount of time is generally deemed to be no more than 3 months unless consideration has been paid to the merchant to extend the time period.

2. Option Contract—In many states, if consideration is received by the offeror to keep the offer open for an agreed period of time, the offer is irrevocable for that period of time and is the subject matter of the option contract. In addition, if the offeree detrimentally, reasonably and foreseeably relies on the offer, this may be deemed a substitute for the required consideration.

3. Unilateral Contract Offers—In many states, offers to make unilateral contracts—contracts in which the offeror warns the offeree that the only way the offeree can accept is by completing performance—are irrevocable for a period of time.

Acceptance of the Offer

Acceptance According to General Contract Law Principles

Under common law contract law, there must be acceptance of the offer, and the offer must not have been terminated prior to the acceptance, in order for a contract to be formed. The contract type dictates the manner in which acceptance must be made.

1. Acceptance Under a Unilateral Contract

A unilateral contract exists when the offeror has clearly warned the offeree that the only way to accept the offer is to completely perform the requested act. Complete performance constitutes acceptance of the offer, at which time the contract is formed.

2. Acceptance Under a Bilateral Contract

A bilateral contract proposes acceptance of an offer by a promise which is made expressly or by conduct.

(a) Express Acceptance—For there to be express acceptance of an offer, there must be both commitment and communication.

(b) Acceptance By Conduct—Acceptance by conduct exists if there has been commencement of performance instead of a promise to perform.

Many states consider that a valid contract has been formed if one accepts the benefit of unsolicited goods. For example, if you mistakenly received a subscription for a magazine and then read the magazine, this may be considered an implied promise to pay for the magazine. Some states, however, would consider unsolicited goods an unconditional gift.

Acceptance Under the Uniform Commercial Code

The offer contained in a contract involving the sale of goods, governed by the UCC, can be accepted by (1) a promise to buy goods, or (2) by performance.

1. Acceptance by a Promise to Buy Goods—A offers to buy corn from B, a farmer. To validly accept A's offer, B can simply call A and promise to send the shipment of corn.

2. Acceptance by Performance—Using the foregoing example, B can also validly accept A's offer by shipping the corn to A, an act which constitutes performance. In addition, there are certain rules which accompany acceptance by performance, as follows:

(a) If performance will take some time, then notice that the performance will take place is required;

(b) Acceptance occurs whether performance consisted of shipping the right goods or the wrong goods. The rationale for this is that we must make the shipment an acceptance of the offer so that there is a valid contract which can be declared to have been breached in order to provide the buyer with a remedy at law against the seller of the non-conforming goods.

Nevertheless, an exception to this rule exists when the seller states that the shipment of non-conforming goods is being sent as an accommodation to the buyer. In this case, the shipment of non-conforming goods is treated as a counter-offer which may or may not be accepted by the buyer.

The counter-offer, as set forth above, in effect rejects the original offer. If the buyer uses the non-conforming goods, he is deemed to have accepted the counter-offer and thus a contract is formed.

Consideration

Consideration is the inducement to enter into a contract. Consideration may involve some right, interest, profit, or benefit which accrues to one party, or some forbearance, detriment, loss or responsibility undertaken by the other party. Simply stated, the consideration is what each party bargains for in the agreement.

Consideration is an essential component of an enforceable contract. There must be at least one consideration supported promise from each party to the contract for consideration to exist.

Adequacy of Consideration

The court generally does not concern itself with the fairness or adequacy of the consideration. However, on occasion, if the consideration appears patently unfair or grossly inadequate, the court may rule that the contract is unenforceable due to unconscionability.

This would be particularly likely where the parties were in unequal bargaining positions or when one party is found to have taken unfair advantage of the other. To avoid such an outcome, the parties to the contract should recite facts which adequately explain why the provision in question is, in fact, fair.

Many agreements contain the following clause: "For $1.00 and other good and valuable consideration, receipt of which is hereby acknowledged, the parties agree as follows. . ." This clause is routinely used as a boilerplate recitation of consideration, whether or not the $1.00 is actually paid.

This type of clause is often used in agreements where the parties wish to keep the actual sale price confidential. Although commonly used, one should be cautioned that the "$1.00 consideration clause" may raise questions as to the inequality of the exchange. It is safer to specify the mutual promises with particularity.

THE AGREEMENT—A MEETING OF THE MINDS

There must be an agreement by both parties as to the subject matter and terms of the contract. There must be mutual assent, i.e. a "meeting of the minds." Nevertheless, a reasonable manifestation of assent may suffice.

CONTRACTUAL CONDITIONS

A condition is a future and uncertain event which must occur, unless it is excused, before performance under a contract becomes due. Conditions may be (1) express; or (2) constructive.

Express conditions

Express conditions are those conditions set forth in the terms of the contract. They modify the promise contained in the contract. They act to either support the duty to perform or prevent performance of the duty.

Enforcement of the duty depends, in part, on the control each party has in meeting the condition. For example, if A agrees to paint B's house, and B agrees to pay A $1,000 if B is satisfied that A has done a good paint job, there exists both a condition and a covenant of good faith on both parties. The conditions are that A provide a good paint job and that B make payment for the paint job. Thus, both parties have control in that they must make a good faith effort to have the event occur.

Constructive Conditions

Constructive conditions occur as follows:

(a) When one party's performance under the contract precedes the other party's performance, the first party's performance is a constructive condition to the second; or

(b) When one party's performance under the contract takes longer than the other party's performance, the longer performance is a constructive condition to the former.

When there is simultaneous performance under the contract, both performances are constructively conditioned concurrently on each other.

Timing of Performance of the Condition

The conditions contained in a contract may be required to be performed at various points in time, as follows:

1. Condition Precedent—A condition precedent is one which must be performed before the agreement becomes effective. A condition precedent requires the occurrence of some event or the performance of some act before the contract is binding on the parties and must be completed before the duty under the contract matures.

2. Condition Concurrent—A condition concurrent exists when the parties to the contract are subject to mutual conditions precedent.

3. Condition Subsequent—A condition subsequent is a provision giving one party the right to divest himself of liability and obligation to perform further if the other party fails to meet the condition. The condition subsequent must occur after the duty. The condition then acts to discharge the duty.

Excusing the Condition

Conditions must be either excused or satisfied in order for the duty to occur. The party whose performance is conditioned must perform regardless in the following situations:

Failure to Cooperate or Prevention of the Occurrence of the Condition

The party whose performance is conditioned must perform regardless of whether there is failure to cooperate, or if there is prevention of the occurrence of the condition.

Anticipatory Repudiation

Anticipatory repudiation occurs when the party whose performance is conditioned repudiates the contract. When a party repudiates the contract, the breach may be accelerated and the condition excused. If repudiation occurs before the other party has performed, the repudiation accelerates the breach and excuses the condition. If the repudiation occurs after the other party has performed, you cannot accelerate the breach.

If a party is unsure whether a breach is coming, he or she may demand adequate assurance that performance will occur. Adequate assurance must be in writing and received within a reasonable amount of time.

Under the UCC, a reasonable time is deemed to be 30 days. If the potentially breaching party fails to respond, then there is a repudiation and all the effects of a repudiation come into play as described above.

Voluntary disablement refers to anticipatory repudiation by conduct. In this case, the repudiating party does something that prevents performance. This operates to excuse all the conditions for performance and accelerates the breach if it occurs before the other party's performance.

Estoppel

Estoppel occurs when the party whose performance is conditioned, prior to the time the event is to occur, states that they don't care whether the event occurs and they will perform anyway. If the other party changes his or her position as a result of this statement, then estoppel occurs and the condition is excused.

Waiver

Waiver occurs when the party whose performance is conditioned on an event that did not occur, thereafter states that he or she will perform anyway. The difference between estoppel and waiver is that estoppel occurs before the condition was to take place and waiver occurs after the condition was to take place.

Satisfying the Condition

If a condition has not been excused, as set forth above, then it must be satisfied in order for the duty to occur. Satisfaction is considered complete if all of the conditions are met. Complete satisfaction is required for all express conditions. Satisfaction is considered substantially complete if all conditions other than express conditions are met.

Under the divisibility doctrine, if there are divisible portions of a contract, you don't have to wait until the entire performance is completed to have the duty arise.

CHAPTER 2:
CONTRACT DUTIES

IN GENERAL

A duty contained in a contract can be discharged, as follows:

1. Modification—Modification is the term used when the parties are changing the duties under the original contract. If a modification is enforceable, then the original duties are discharged and new duties arise based on the modification. For example:

> Original Duty—Buyer agrees to buy a television from Seller on January 1st for $1000.

> Modification—Buyer and Seller agree that Buyer will instead buy the television from Seller on February 1st for $900.

> Outcome—The duty to deliver changed from January 1st to February 1st and the duty to pay $1000 changed from $1000 to $900.

2. Mutual Rescission/Cancellation/Release—If there is mutual rescission, cancellation or release of the duties contained in the contract, this eliminates the requirement of performance of those duties.

> For example, Buyer agrees to buy a television and VCR from Seller at individually stated prices. Buyer thereafter says he only wants to buy the VCR and Seller agrees. This eliminates both the duty to deliver and the duty to pay for the television.

3. Accord and Satisfaction—Accord and satisfaction occurs when the parties to the original contract resolve a dispute existing in the contract and make a new agreement to satisfy the dispute. The accord, i.e., the new agreement, does not in itself eliminate the duties under the old contract. It is the satisfaction—the performance under the new agreement—that eliminates the duties under the old contract. If there is no satisfaction, i.e., performance of the accord, then a lawsuit can be brought to enforce the terms of the original contract.

4. Novation—A novation involves the substitution of a new party and new performance in place of the old party and old performance. A no-

vation is not an assignment or delegation because neither party unilaterally introduces a third party into the contract. In a novation, all three parties agree. Because all parties agreed, the old party can never be sued nor sue on the original contract.

5. Impossibility—Impossibility means that the contract cannot be performed at all by anyone because of an event that has occurred, in which case all duties are discharged and nobody can be sued. Impossibility occurs if the subject matter of the contract has been destroyed before performance, e.g.:

(a) A contract to prune trees is entered into, however, before there is performance, the trees are uprooted in a storm and destroyed.

(b) In a contract for personal services, if the performer dies or is otherwise incapacitated,the duty to perform is discharged.

(c) In a supplier contract, if the sole source of the supply is destroyed, the duty to perform is discharged.

(d) If there is a supervening illegality wherein a law is passed that says the parties are no longer permitted to do the act which the contract required, the duty to perform is discharged.

Under the UCC, impossibility is termed "casualty to identified goods." Casualty to identified goods e.g., when goods are destroyed, operates to discharge the duties under the contract. The casualty must occur before the "risk of loss" has passed from seller to buyer. Risk of loss is further discussed below.

Identified goods are those which are either:

1. Identified in the contract; or

2. Marked, shipped or otherwise designated as the goods under the contract.

Under the UCC, if there is a single delivery of goods, the duty to deliver must be undertaken perfectly. Nevertheless, the UCC provides that if tender is not perfect, the seller has the right to cure tender anytime up to the agreed upon time of performance.

6. Impracticability—Impracticability occurs when a party can't perform at the time because of some unforeseen, severe and unassumed event that makes it unreasonable to perform as written in the contract. If the event which makes performance impracticable is temporary, the duties are merely suspended until the event ceases, at which time the duties to perform arise promptly. If the event which makes performance impracticable is permanent, then it is likened to impossibility and there is a discharge of duties.

7. Frustration—Frustration occurs when the purpose of the contract no longer exists. Therefore, if some unforeseen event acts to cancel the purpose of the contract, and both parties knew of the purpose of the contract, then all duties are discharged.

8. Failure to Excuse or Satisfy a Condition Subsequent—Chronologically, this occurs after the duty to perform occurs. The duty must be excused or satisfied. If the duty is not excused or satisfied, the duty is alive and must be performed or a breach occurs.

Risk of Loss

Risk of loss refers to the set of rules that govern in determining the party liable for goods involved in a sale should they be damaged or lost at some point during the transfer from seller to buyer. In general, risk of loss passes from the seller to the buyer when the seller has completed performance under the contract, as follows:

1. Face-to-Face Delivery—If the seller is a merchant, the risk of loss passes upon physical receipt of the goods by the buyer. However, if the seller is not a merchant, then risk of loss occurs when tender of delivery occurs. For example, tender occurs when the seller notifies the buyer that the goods are available and makes the goods available to the buyer.

2. Delivery by Intermediary or Carrier—The risk of loss depends on how the goods are shipped:

a) FOB—free on board—to a stated destination, e.g. FOB New York. This means that the goods will be priced so freight to the destination is included. If the goods are sent FOB to a place other than where the seller is, it is known as a destination contract and the seller has an obligation to get the goods to the place and tender delivery by notice of availability and holding the goods for a reasonable time.

If the goods are damaged or lost either before they reach the destination, or before the goods are at the destination for a reasonable time, the duties are discharged. However, if the goods are at the destination for a reasonable time after buyer is notified, and they are lost or damaged, it is the buyer's problem and he must pay for the goods anyway.

b) FAS—free along side—Port—This means that the price of the goods includes delivery to the port or ship.

c) CIF (cost-insurance-freight) Port

d) C&F (cost and freight) Port

For all of the above examples except FOB to a destination other than where the seller is, the general risk of loss rule is that the risk of loss will pass when the Seller delivers the goods to the carrier and makes a reasonable contract for their delivery. This ends the seller's responsibility.

Casualty to identified goods e.g., when goods are destroyed, operates to discharge the duties under the contract. The casualty must occur before the risk of loss has passed from seller to buyer. Identified goods are those which are either:

1. Identified in the contract; or

2. Marked, shipped or otherwise designated as the goods under the contract.

If there is casualty before delivery of the goods to the carrier, then the duties are discharged. However, if there is casualty after delivery of the goods to the carrier, it is the Buyer's problem and he still must pay for the goods.

Where partial casualty of the shipment occurs, the buyer has the option of either (1) treating the contract as terminated; or (2) electing to take the goods with a price adjustment.

CHAPTER 3:
CONTRACT INTERPRETATION

PARTIES

According to the Restatement Second of the Law of Contracts, and as further provided in the Uniform Commercial Code, in choosing among the reasonable meanings of a promise or agreement or a term thereof, the meaning that is generally preferred is one which operates against the party who supplies the words or from whom a writing otherwise proceeds.

See Section 206 of the Restatement Second of the Law of Contracts set forth at Appendix 1.

The rationale for this provision is that where one party chooses the terms of a contract, he is likely to provide more carefully for the protection of his own interests than for those of the other party. He is also more likely than the other party to have reason to know of uncertainties of the meaning. Indeed, he may leave a meaning deliberately obscure, intending to decide at a later date what meaning to assert.

In cases of doubt, therefore, so long as other factors are not decisive, there is substantial reason for preferring the meaning of the other party. The rule is often invoked in cases of standardized contracts and in cases where the drafting party has the stronger bargaining position.

The rule that language is interpreted against the party who chose it has no direct application to cases where the language is prescribed by law, as is sometimes true with respect to insurance policies, bills of lading and other standardized documents.

THE PAROL EVIDENCE RULE

The Parol Evidence Rule seeks to preserve the integrity of written agreements by refusing to permit contracting parties to attempt to alter their written contract through the use of contemporaneous parol—i.e., oral—declarations. The purpose of the Parol Evidence Rule is to provide the parties to the contract some certainty as to their rights and obligations under the contract.

Thus, if the parties have a final written agreement, then no prior oral or written negotiations, or contemporaneous oral negotiations, may be introduced into evidence, to vary or contradict the terms of the final written agreement. All previous oral agreements merge in the writing and the terms of the writing control.

The only exception would be a showing of fraud, duress, mistake, undue influence, incapacity or illegality, in which case parol evidence would be admissible. In addition, if an agreement is ambiguous on a certain point, parol evidence is admissible to explain the ambiguity.

To determine whether an agreement is, in fact, final, the following factors must be considered:

1. The language of the agreement states that it is final, e.g., there is a merger or integration clause in the agreement.

2. Where the agreement is silent as to finality, the court must examine both the agreement and the parol evidence and decide according to the standard of whether a reasonable person similarly situated would have put the parol evidence into the agreement.

If the answer is yes, then the parol evidence is not admissible and the contract is determined to be final. If the answer is no, then the parol evidence is admissible and the contract is considered to be only partially integrated. In that case, a collateral oral agreement is admissible and, if established, enforceable.

Thus, all relevant evidence is admissible to determine the issue of finality, including the parol evidence. Parol evidence only covers prior or contemporaneous evidence. Any evidence which occurred subsequent to the agreement, even if it varies or contradicts the terms of the agreement, is admissible.

State and local laws vary, however, some states have enacted statutes which provide that a contract cannot be changed except by a subsequent written agreement.

The Parol Evidence Rule Under the Uniform Commercial Code

Section 2-202 of the UCC sets forth the Code's version of the Parol Evidence Rule, which states that the terms of a final written agreement, or confirmatory memoranda between the parties, may not be contradicted by evidence of any prior agreement or contemporaneous oral agreement.

Exceptions

The UCC does allow the parties to explain or supplement the writing by introducing evidence involving:

Course of Dealing—Course of dealing refers to the sequence of previous conduct between the parties to a particular transaction which is fairly to be regarded as establishing a common basis of understanding for interpreting their expressions and other conduct (UCC Section 1-205(1));

Usage of Trade—Usage of trade refers to any practice or method of dealing having such regularity of observance in a place, vocation or trade as to justify an expectation that it will be observed with respect to the transaction in question (UCC Section 1-205(2)).

Course of Performance—Course of performance shall be relevant where the contract for sale involves repeated occasions for performance by either party with knowledge of the nature of the performance and opportunity for objection to it by the other, where such course of performance was accepted or acquiesced in without objection (UCC Section 2-208(1)).

CHAPTER 4:
CONTRACT FORMATION DEFENSES

IN GENERAL

A contract is generally enforceable if all of the conditions for forming a valid contract have been met, as set forth above. However, under certain defined circumstances, there may exist a defense to enforcing the contract. The most common defenses to formation of a valid contract are:

1. Formation Defects

A formation defect may occur if one of the essential elements are missing, such as the offer, acceptance, consideration, or mutual agreement.

2. Statute of Frauds

The statute of frauds generally requires that certain defined contracts must be in writing to be enforceable. The statute of frauds is more fully discussed below.

3. Incapacity

Incapacity is generally defined as the lack of legal ability to act due to diminished or absent physical or intellectual power, such as mental incompetency or intoxication; or a natural or legal disqualification, such as age. A contract is unenforceable against—and voidable by—a party who lacked the capacity to enter into the contract.

4. Illegality

Illegality is defined as that which is contrary to the principles of law. An illegal contract may exist if either the subject matter or the purpose of the contract is illegal.

Certain contracts may have an element of illegality in them yet still be enforceable. For example, if one obtains a loan from a finance company, and the loan company charges interest at a rate which is higher than the legal interest rate—a practice known as usury—a court may still uphold the contract, but will reform it by lowering the illegal interest rate so as to uphold the bargain and enforce the contract.

5. Misrepresentation/Fraud

Misrepresentation is defined as any manifestation by words or other conduct, by one person to another, that under the circumstances amounts to an assertion that is not in accordance with the facts. A misrepresentation which justifies the rescission of a contract is a false statement of a substantive fact which is material to the proper understanding of the matter in hand, and which was made with the intent to deceive or mislead. The misrepresentation defense may involve either fraud in the inducement to enter into the contract, or fraud in the execution of the contract.

Nondisclosure is also a type of fraud which occurs when a person fails to disclose a fact known to him, when he knows that disclosure would correct a misunderstanding of the other party as to a basic assumption of the contract. Non-disclosure of a fact may be taken as an assertion that the fact does not exist. The court would likely find that there has been bad faith dealing on the non-disclosing party.

6. Duress

Duress is defined as a condition where one is induced, by the wrongful act or threat of another, to enter into a contract under circumstances which would deprive that person of his or her exercise of free will. A contract induced by duress is unenforceable and may be either void or voidable.

Duress may occur either personally—e.g., when the person is literally forced to enter into the contract—or economically—e.g., when one party tries to take advantage of another party's unfortunate financial situation. Nevertheless, economic duress cannot be used as a defense to the enforceability of a contract unless the party taking advantage of the situation has also caused the negative economic condition.

7. Unconscionability

The defense of unconscionability applies to all contracts. Unconscionability refers to an absence of meaningful choice on the part of one of the contracting parties, together with contract terms which are unreasonably favorable to the other contracting party. Unconscionability is more fully discussed below.

8. Mistake

Mistake exists when a person does something, or fails to do something, due to some erroneous conviction of law or fact. A mistake may occur (a) mutually; (b) unilaterally; or (c) due to the ambiguity of a material term, as set forth below.

(a) Mutual Mistake - A mutual mistake occurs when the parties to the contract agree upon a subject matter that does not exist. Such a contract is void. For example, an antique dealer sells what he believes to be a genuine Louis XIV chair to a collector. The collector thereafter discovers that the chair is, in fact, a replica. This is a mutual mistake by both parties to the contract, therefore, the contract is void.

(b) Unilateral Mistake - A unilateral mistake occurs when one party to the contract makes a mistake as to a term of the contract. Such a contract is fully enforceable unless the other party knew or should have known that the mistake was being made.

(c) Ambiguous Material Term - If the contract contains an ambiguous material term, i.e., a term which can be interpreted in more than one way, the contract is unenforceable unless both parties agree that they intended the same meaning for the ambiguous term. However, if one of the parties to the contract was aware of the ambiguity, and the other party was unaware of the ambiguity, the contract may be enforced according to the understanding of the "innocent" party.

THE STATUTE OF FRAUDS

The Statute of Frauds, also known as the *Statute of Frauds and Perjuries*, is derived from a 1677 English statute which was modified and adopted by almost all of jurisdictions. It prohibits the initiation of lawsuits based on certain categories of contracts, unless the particular contract is substantiated by a writing which was signed by the party to be charged, or the party's authorized agent.

The purpose of the statute of frauds was to combat fraud and perjury in the making of contracts. It is designed to protect certain contracts which are deemed to be so valuable, or so easily imagined, that the party's word alone is not sufficient to enforce the contract. The statute of frauds does not make a contract void, however, it does make the contract either voidable or enforceable dependent upon the tangible evidence which is submitted.

Types of Contracts Protected by the Statute of Frauds

Examples of the types of contracts which may be protected under the Statute of Frauds, depending on the applicable state laws, include (1) a contract involving insurance; (2) a contract for a commission or finder's fee; (3) a contract where marriage is the consideration, e.g. a prenuptial agreement; (4) a contract to answer for the debt of another; (5) a contract involving real property interests; (6) a contract for the sale of goods over $500; and (7) a contract that cannot be completed within one year after formation.

Kinds of Tangible Evidence Necessary For Enforceability

The following evidence would likely be probative of an enforceable agreement:

1. Any kind of a signed, written statement which adequately specifies the essential terms of the contract is sufficient to substantiate that a contract existed. Specifically, the writing should contain the following:

(a) Identification of the parties to the contract;

(b) A description of the subject matter of the contract;

(c) A description of the consideration for the contract; and

(d) The signature of the party to be charged.

2. Partial or Full Performance Under the Contract

Partial or full performance under the contract by one of the parties may be tangible evidence of the existence of a contract, as follows:

(a) If there has been partial performance, the contract will be enforceable to the extent of the performance.

(b) If there has been full performance, the contract will be fully enforceable.

The Statute of Frauds Under the Uniform Commercial Code

Section 2-201 of the UCC sets forth the Code's statute of frauds, which requires that there be some writing sufficient to indicate that a contract for the sale of goods was entered into by the parties, and signed by the party against whom enforcement is sought.

The statute applies to the sale of goods with a value of $500 or over. The writing must recite a quantity term. If such a writing is produced, the contract may be enforced, but only for the quantity of goods shown in the writing.

Notwithstanding the foregoing requirements pertaining to the sufficiency of the writing, UCC Section 2-201 also states that a written confirmation between merchants, which is signed by the sender, and which recites a quantity term, need not be signed by the party to be charged in order to be enforceable. If the receiving party does not want the goods, it is incumbent upon him to send a written notice of objection to the seller within 10 days after the written confirmation is received.

Exceptions

UCC Section 2-201 also sets forth the exceptions to the writing requirement. If the contract does not satisfy the writing requirement, it may still be valid and enforceable under the following conditions:

1. If the goods are specially manufactured for the buyer and the seller has substantially begun production or procurement of the goods prior to receiving a notice of repudiation from the buyer; or

2. If the party who is being charged makes an admission in court, by pleadings, testimony or otherwise, that a contract for sale was made; or

3. If the goods have been received and accepted, or if payment for the goods has been made and accepted.

UNCONSCIONABILITY

Unconscionability refers to an absence of meaningful choice on the part of one of the contracting parties, together with contract terms which are unreasonably favorable to the other contracting party. The defense of unconscionability applies to all contracts.

Unconscionability Under the Uniform Commercial Code

Section 2-302 of the UCC sets forth the Code's definition of unconscionability which states that a contract may not be enforced if the court finds the contract, or any clause of the contract, to have been unconscionable at the time it was made.

The court also has the option of enforcing the remainder of the contract without the unconscionable clause, or placing a limitation on the unconscionable clause to avoid an unconscionable result from its application. The parties to the contract are permitted to introduce evidence to show that the contract, or clause of the contract, are not unconscionable.

The Determination of Unconscionability

Unconscionability is often found where one of the parties to the contract has the stronger bargaining power, and uses it to pressure the other party to agree to unfair terms. Like the obligation of good faith and fair dealing set forth in Section 205 of the Restatement, the policy against unconscionable contracts or terms applies to a wide variety of types of conduct. The determination that a contract or term is or is not unconscionable is made in the light of its setting, purpose and effect.

Relevant factors include weaknesses in the contracting process like those involved in more specific rules as to contractual capacity, fraud, and other invalidating causes. The policy also overlaps with rules which render particular bargains or terms unenforceable on grounds of public policy.

Policing against unconscionable contracts or terms has sometimes been accomplished "by adverse construction of language, by manipulation of the rules of offer and acceptance or by determinations that the clause is contrary to public policy or to the dominant purpose of the contract.

Traditionally, a bargain was said to be unconscionable in an action at law if it was "such as no man in his senses and not under delusion would make on the one hand, and as no honest and fair man would accept on the other. Damages were limited to those to which the aggrieved party was "equitably" entitled.

Even though a contract was fully enforceable in an action for damages, equitable remedies such as specific performance were refused where "the sum total of its provisions drives too hard a bargain for a court of conscience to assist."

Modern procedural reforms have blurred the distinction between remedies at law and in equity. For contracts for the sale of goods, the Uniform Commercial Code does not distinguish between law and equity and adds, in Comment 1 to §2-302, that: "The principle is one of the prevention of oppression and unfair surprise and not of disturbance of allocation of risks because of superior bargaining power."

Inadequacy of consideration does not of itself invalidate a bargain, but gross disparity in the values exchanged may be an important factor in a determination that a contract is unconscionable and may be sufficient ground, without more, for denying specific performance. Such a disparity may also corroborate indications of defects in the bargaining process, or may affect the remedy to be granted when there is a violation of a more specific rule.

Theoretically it is possible for a contract to be oppressive taken as a whole, even though there is no weakness in the bargaining process and no single term which is in itself unconscionable. Ordinarily, however, an unconscionable contract involves other factors as well as overall imbalance.

On the other hand, particular terms may be unconscionable whether or not the contract as a whole is unconscionable. Some types of terms are not enforced, regardless of context, such as provisions for unreasonably large liquidated damages, or limitations on a debtor's right to redeem collateral.

Other terms may be unconscionable in some contexts but not in others. Overall imbalance and weaknesses in the bargaining process are then important.

A determination that a contract or term is unconscionable is made by the court in the light of all the material facts. Under the Uniform Commercial Code, the determination is made "as a matter of law," but the parties are to be afforded an opportunity to present evidence as to commercial setting, purpose and effect to aid the court in its determination.

Incidental findings of fact are made by the court rather than by a jury, but are accorded the usual weight given to such findings of fact in appellate review. An appellate court will also consider whether proper standards were applied.

Remedies

The simplest remedy to enforce the policy against unconscionable agreements is the denial of specific performance where the contract as a whole was unconscionable when made. If such a contract is entirely executory, denial of money damages may also be appropriate. But the policy is not penal. Unless the parties can be restored to their pre-contract positions, the offending party will ordinarily be awarded at least the reasonable value of performance rendered by him.

Where a term rather than the entire contract is unconscionable, the appropriate remedy is ordinarily to deny effect to the unconscionable term. In such cases as that of an exculpatory term, the effect may be to enlarge the liability of the offending party.

Unconscionable at Formation

To be deemed unconscionable, the contract must have been unfair and oppressive to one of the parties under the terms existing at the time the contract was formed.

According to the Restatement Second of the Law of Contracts, and as further provided in the Uniform Commercial Code, if a contract or term thereof is unconscionable at the time the contract is made a court may refuse to enforce the contract, or may enforce the remainder of the contract without the unconscionable term, or may so limit the application of any unconscionable term as to avoid any unconscionable result.

However, the court may find the contract enforceable because although the deal may appear unfair under the present economic conditions, the terms of the contract were fair at the time the parties entered into the contract.

Standardized Agreements

Standardized agreements often contain potentially unconscionable provisions which are set forth in fine print or located inconspicuously within the document. Such contracts are often referred to as contracts of adhesion. A contract of adhesion is not unconscionable per se, and all unconscionable contracts are not contracts of adhesion. Nonetheless, the more standardized the agreement and the less a party may bargain meaningfully, the more susceptible the contract, or a clause of a contract, will be to a claim of unconscionability.

To avoid a finding of unconscionability, provisions which appear potentially unconscionable should be set forth in plain language and set apart from the rest of the contract, such as in bold or highlighted print.

Plain Language Laws

Most people have been confronted with a contractual document that contained numerous paragraphs of fine print legalese. Such language is common in standard form contracts, such as leases and consumer credit agreements.

This creates a dilemma for the layperson because such transactions are not commonly those for which expending legal fees are desirable. Therefore, most people make an attempt at deciphering the contract language without legal guidance, and end up signing without a complete understanding of the agreement.

Largely due to the consumer activist movement, various state legislatures have attempted to address this problem by enacting "Plain Language" laws which require that certain consumer contracts be written so that the average layperson can understand them.

The two general categories of plain language laws which have been enacted are the (1) general/subjective plain language laws; and the (2) specific/objective plain language laws.

General/Subjective Plain Language Laws

The general/subjective plain language laws require the drafter to ensure the language contained in the contract is sufficiently clear, containing common usage words, so that the layperson can understand what they are signing. In addition, the layout of the contract is generally required to be clearly set forth, with its various sections appropriately labeled and subdivided.

Specific/Objective Plain Language Laws

The specific/objective plain language laws set forth an elaborate scoring system which must be adhered to in order to be deemed acceptable. A common objective test used in specific/objective plain language statutes is known as the Flesch test of reading ease.

The Flesch test computes a score based on the measurement of the number of syllables in each word and the number of words in each sentence. The theory behind this objective test is that shorter words in shorter sentences are more easily understood. In addition to the Flesch test, there are certain specific requirements concerning the size of the type and layout of the contract.

Consumer Protection Acts

Most jurisdictions have enacted Consumer Protection Acts to protect consumers from unfair or deceptive acts or practices, such as unconscionable, illegal and unenforceable provisions often hidden within standardized consumer credit contracts. Consumer Protection Acts confer liability upon the violators of the provisions of the Acts.

A Directory of Consumer Protection Agencies is set forth at Appendix 2.

CHAPTER 5:
BREACH OF CONTRACT AND REMEDIES

IN GENERAL

A breach of contract occurs when one has an absolute duty to perform under a contract but fails to perform even though performance was not excused. The remedies for breach of contract differ depending on whether or not the contract was governed by the UCC.

BREACH UNDER NON-UCC CONTRACTS

The remedies for breach of a non-UCC contract are basically (1) money damages; and (2) specific performance, where feasible.

Money Damages

Damages are defined as the pecuniary compensation or indemnity which may be recovered in court by any person who has suffered loss, detriment, or injury, whether to his person, property or rights, through the unlawful act or omission or negligence of another.

In general, the measure of damages for a breach of contract is to put the non-breaching party in as good a position as if the breach had not occurred and performance had been completed. Liquidated damages are those damages which were negotiated and agreed to in the contract. Mitigation refers to the deduction of damages which could have been mitigated by the non-breaching party.

Specific Performance

Specific performance is a remedy available to an aggrieved party who would not be adequately made whole with money damages. Instead, the party wants the contract enforced. Whenever the subject matter of the contract is unique, such as real property, specific performance is an authorized equitable remedy which the court can award at its own discretion.

Although they can be considered unique, personal services contracts—such as an entertainment contract—cannot be specifically performed. However, the non-breaching party may be able to get an injunction, i.e. a court order that would prevent the breaching party from performing elsewhere, during the term of the contract that was breached.

BREACH OF CONTRACT UNDER THE UNIFORM COMMERCIAL CODE

The remedies available for breach of contract under the UCC are similar to non-UCC remedies, however, they are given different labels.

Seller's "Status Quo" Remedies

1. If during manufacture, seller manufactures and buyer breaches, seller is entitled to do anything reasonable, e.g. continue to manufacture the goods and sell them as finished products;

2. If the seller has shipped goods in transit to buyer and buyer breaches, seller can stop the goods in transit. If the buyer is insolvent, this rule applies to all goods so that they won't be delivered and fall into the hands of the buyer's creditors. However, if buyer is merely breaching, then the seller can only stop large shipments.

3. If the goods are already delivered, and the buyer breaches, if the buyer is insolvent, the seller may reclaim the goods within 10 days after delivery. If the buyer is not insolvent, the seller must sue for breach of contract.

Seller's "Right of Resale" Remedies

1. The seller has the right to find a substitute buyer to buy the goods. To exercise that right, the seller is required to give the buyer notice of intention to resell the goods. That notice is excused if the goods are of the type that will perish or decline rapidly. The seller must also make a commercially reasonable resale. If there is a resale, the seller is entitled to recover the difference between the contract price and the resale price from the buyer.

2. If there is no resale, the seller can get a market price recovery standard of damages, which would be the difference between the contract price and the market price for the goods at the time and place of tender.

3. Sellers who sell goods for the same price all of the time and who, therefore, experience no change in market price, rendering the above two remedies ineffective, can sue the buyer for the profit they would have made on the sale. This is referred to as lost volume sales.

4. Seller can sue the buyer for the price of the goods whenever the goods are so unique that there is no resale value or market price. The seller will

then give the buyer the goods. This is similar to specific performance in non-UCC contracts.

Buyer's "Status Quo" Remedies

1. The buyer can reject nonconforming goods anytime before the buyer accepts the goods.

2. The buyer can revoke acceptance of the goods if the buyer thereafter realizes that there is a defect with the goods. However, the defect must be substantial because acceptance has already been taken. In addition, the defect must have been difficult to discover.

Buyer's Procedures to Exercise Remedies

1. The buyer must give the seller notice of the defect. Once the notice is given, the buyer must wait for seller's instructions. If seller gives reasonable instructions, buyer must follow them. However, if the seller does not give any instructions, or gives unreasonable instructions, then the buyer can do anything reasonable with the goods at the seller's expense—e.g. sell the goods, return the goods, etc.

2. The buyer must attempt to cover his losses,i.e., the buyer must go out into the market place without unreasonable delay to buy a reasonable substitute for the goods. If the buyer does that, he is entitled to receive the difference between the cost of covering the goods, and the contract price, so that the buyer is made "whole."

3. To determine a market price recovery, the buyer gets the difference between the market price when the buyer learns of the breach and the contract price.

4. Whenever the subject matter of the contract is unique, the Buyer can sue the seller to require that the goods be delivered.

CHAPTER 6:
WARRANTIES

There are three basic types of warranties upon which a consumer relies: (1) Express Warranty; (2) Implied Warranty of Merchantability; and (3) Implied Warranty of Fitness for a Particular Purpose.

EXPRESS WARRANTY

An express warranty includes oral or written promises by the seller that the product will perform in a certain manner, or that the product conforms to its description.

Under UCC Section 2-313, an express warranty is any affirmation of fact, description or sample furnished by the seller to the buyer that relates to the goods and becomes part of the basis of the bargain. Thus, it is expressly warranted that the product will conform to such affirmation, description or sample.

Further, it is not necessary that the warranty be reduced to writing, nor that any particular words be used, such as "guarantee," in order to create the obligation, as long as the representations were meant to be factual and not mere opinion.

In bringing a claim for breach of an express warranty, a thorough search of all product-related advertising, packaging and promotional items should be accomplished to either (a) uncover and demonstrate the warranty in the case of the plaintiff, or (b) in the case of the defendant, to show that there were no express warranties concerning the product.

In pursuing a claim under breach of express warranty, the burden of proof lies with the plaintiff to establish that:

1. The defendant made an express representation relative to the product;

2. The plaintiff knew about the representation; and

3. The plaintiff relied on the representation to his or her detriment.

Depending on the jurisdiction, local statutes may have additional requirements, e.g., timely notice of the breach to the defendant.

IMPLIED WARRANTY OF MERCHANTABILITY

An implied warranty of merchantability is an implied representation that the product is free of defects and meets the general standards of acceptability.

For example, a pair of shoes should last for more than one week. If they fall apart before that time, with normal use, they are unacceptable.

According to UCC Section 2-316, a warranty of merchantability is implied in a contract of sale if the seller is considered a merchant in goods of that type, unless the implied warranty is excluded or modified. Under this section, merchantable goods are those which:

1. Pass without objection in the trade;

2. Are of fair average quality;

3. Are fit for the ordinary purposes for which such goods are used;

4. Are of uniform kind, quality, and quantity within each unit or shipment;

5. Are adequately contained, packaged, and labeled; and

6. Conform to any express warranty given on the container or label.

Because a breach of implied warranty of merchantability results in an unacceptable product, it is unnecessary to prove reliance by the customer on either express or implied representations of the defendant. The unacceptable product itself forms the basis of the breach.

In pursuing a claim under breach of implied warranty of merchantability, the burden of proof lies with the plaintiff to establish the following elements:

1. There must be a sale or other surrender of the product for some type of consideration, such as a lease.

2. The defendant must be a dealer in goods of that type in the regular course of his or her business.

3. There must be a defect, such as a design, manufacturing, or warning defect, which renders the product unsuitable for its ordinary purpose.

Depending on the jurisdiction, local statutes may have additional requirements, e.g., timely notice of the product defect to the defendant.

IMPLIED WARRANTY OF FITNESS FOR A PARTICULAR PURPOSE

As the name demonstrates, this warranty includes the obligation that the product meets the needs of a particular purpose. For example, a certain shoe may be advertised as reliable for mountain climbing. However, if the shoe falls apart during the activity, this would constitute a breach of warranty of fitness for the particular purpose of mountain climbing.

Thus, although a product may be merchantable, it still may be a breach of the implied warranty of fitness for a particular purpose.

In pursuing a claim under breach of implied warranty of fitness, the burden of proof lies with the plaintiff to establish the following elements:

1. A communication from the buyer to the seller of the specific, intended purpose for which the product is being purchased;

2. The plaintiff's injury must arise while in use for that specific purpose;

3. The plaintiff must have relied on the defendant's expertise in selecting the particular product for its intended purpose;

Further, the defendant need not be a dealer in goods of that type in the regular course of his or her business.

CHAPTER 7:
UNFAIR AND DECEPTIVE ACTS AND PRACTICES—LIABILITY BETWEEN CONSUMERS AND SELLERS OF GOODS AND SERVICES

IN GENERAL

All jurisdictions have enacted some sort of legislation which is aimed at protecting consumers from unfair and deceptive acts and practices by sellers of goods and services in the marketplace.

The list of state statutes governing unfair and deceptive acts and practices are set forth at Appendix 3.

Most of the state statutes have utilized the language set forth in Section 5(a)(1) of the Federal Trade Commission Act (the "FTC Act"), which prohibits unfair or deceptive acts or practices and unfair methods of competition. These statutes have various names according to the jurisdiction, such as consumer protection statutes, unfair trade statutes, etc. For the purposes of this Chapter, such statutes will be referred to as state consumer protection statutes.

Many commentators also term these statutes broadly as "Little FTC Acts," although that title is somewhat of a misnomer because not all of the states have adopted every provision of the FTC Act.

THE UNFAIR OR DECEPTIVE PRACTICE

In order to prevail in a lawsuit, one must be able to demonstrate that a particular act or practice is unfair or deceptive. Before making a decision to proceed, one must determine whether the act or practice complained of is prohibited by the consumer protection statutes of the applicable jurisdiction. A careful examination of the statute is crucial because the consumer generally has the burden of proving that the statute applies.

For example, when a consumer protection statute is silent on the definition of particular term, e.g. goods, the jurisdiction's case law may offer further guidance. In addition, the statute itself may refer the reader to the applicable sections of the Uniform Commercial Code for a definition of the term.

The Per Se Violation

A per se violation is a violation which automatically occurs when a practice clearly violates a specific statutory guideline. Most state consumer protection statutes set forth enumerated statutory violations as well as a catchall provision for all other unfair or deceptive acts or practices.

It is preferable to demonstrate to the court that the act is a per se violation rather than leave it up to the court to determine whether it falls within the catchall provision. If a per se violation is demonstrated, the court need only consider whether the act falls within the specific guidelines of the consumer protection statute.

Nevertheless, even if the act appears to be a per se violation, it is wise to additionally plead that the particular act or practice is generally unfair and/or deceptive in case the court finds that the act does not precisely fit within the statute's enumerated provisions. In that case, if the complaint does not contain such a general allegation, the case would likely be dismissed

Again, see the list of state statutes governing unfair and deceptive acts and practices set forth at Appendix 3.

The Non Per Se Violation

Even if a particular act or practice does not violate one of the enumerated prohibitions of the state consumer protection statute, it may nonetheless be a violation. In such a case, the consumer must demonstrate liability to the court.

This may be accomplished by setting forth a detailed account of the unfair and/or deceptive acts or practices, stating favorable precedential case law concerning similar complaints, and showing how the practice violates the general standards of deception or unfairness.

Further, because most state consumer protection statutes are modeled after the Federal Trade Commission Act, one may look to the Act, and cases decided under the Act, for guidance in determining whether a particular act or practice is prohibited.

COMMON LAW FRAUD

Under the common law, a claim arising from a deceptive act or practice would be brought under common law fraud provisions. Common law fraud required the showing of the following elements by clear and convincing evidence:

1. A false representation, usually of fact;

2. Reliance on the representation by the plaintiff;

3. Damage or harm resulting from the reliance;

4. The defendant's knowledge of the falsity of the representation, referred to as *scienter*; and

5. Defendant's intentional misrepresentation in order to gain reliance.

DECEPTION UNDER THE FTC ACT

After the enactment of the FTC Act, and the case law which followed concerning the issue of deception, the above proof requirements were substantially eliminated. The FTC Act did away with the requirements of actual deception, actual reliance, damage, scienter and intent.

Presently, the general standard of proof requires nothing more than a showing that the practice has a tendency or capacity to deceive a significant minority of consumers by a preponderance of the evidence.

EXAMPLES OF UNFAIR OR DECEPTIVE PRACTICES

Following are examples of unfair or deceptive practices for which state consumer protection statutes may provide a remedy to an aggrieved consumer. The reader should be aware that statute provisions vary according to the jurisdiction and one must carefully review the provisions of the consumer protection statute of one's jurisdiction before proceeding with a lawsuit.

Automobile Repairs

Repair shops are often required to provide consumers with written estimates before proceeding with the repairs. Consumers are entitled to inspect parts which were replaced. Padding bills for parts which are not used, or repairs which are not done is a violation.

Automobile Sales

Those engaged in the business of selling automobiles are subject to numerous state and federal laws, such as state lemon laws, the federal

Magnuson-Moss Warranty Act, the federal Odometer Act, and Article 2 of the Uniform Commercial Code. In addition, however, an aggrieved consumer may also find a remedy within the state's consumer protection statute prohibiting unfair and deceptive acts and practices.

For example, it is a violation, among other things, to misrepresent or fail to disclose the prior use of the vehicle; to tamper with the odometer; or to fail to disclose any safety or material defects in the car, etc.

Debt Collection

As more fully set forth in this almanac, those engaged in the collection of debts are subject to the federal Fair Debt Collection Practices Act, as well as state statutes and common law tort principles. However, a consumer may also find available remedies in the state consumer protection statute prohibiting unfair and deceptive acts and practices.

In general, if unfair debt collection comes within the ambit of the state statute, the provisions generally prohibit conduct including harassment of the debtor; misrepresentation as to the nature and identity of the debt collector; and misrepresentations as to the imminency of legal action or the legal consequences of non-payment, etc.

Landlord-Tenant Matters

State consumer protection statutes may also be a source of redress against unfair dealings with one's landlord. For example, landlords must disclose the tenant's right to his or her security deposit and must itemize any claims made against the security deposit; lease agreements must be readable by the tenant; landlords may not make an unreasonable entry onto the tenant's premises; and, the landlord may not evict a tenant in retaliation for making complaints against the landlord.

Encyclopedia Sales

It may be a violation of the state consumer protection statute for an encyclopedia salesman to misrepresent their reasons for contacting the potential purchaser. For example, the salesman cannot fool the buyer into believing he or she won a prize in order to gain access.

Unsolicited Goods

It may be a violation of the state consumer protection statute to deliver unsolicited consumer goods and then charge the consumer.

Future Service Contracts

A future service contract refers to an agreement whereby the consumer agrees to pay for services which are to be rendered in the future over a period of time. Violations of the state consumer protection statute may occur if, for example, misrepresentations are made as to the consumer's ability to cancel the contract; or if large penalties are assessed upon cancellation, etc.

Burial Services

In addition to the provisions set forth in the federal Funeral Practices Trade Regulation Rule, state consumer protection statutes may provide additional remedies. Prohibited practices include misrepresentations concerning the legal requirements of the process; and failure to provide itemized price information, etc.

POTENTIAL DEFENDANTS

In bringing a lawsuit for a violation of the state's consumer protection statute, one must decide which parties to name as defendants. The most common defendants include the principal—e.g., a corporation; its agents; corporate officers, directors and shareholders; and partners, as set forth below.

The principal is liable for the acts of its agents, including its employees. However, the principal is not generally held liable for true independent contractors. If faced with this situation, one must carefully examine the relationship between the principal and the independent contractor to see whether a principal/agent relationship existed instead.

The officers, directors and shareholders of a corporation would be liable to the consumer if they were directly involved in the deceptive practice. In addition, if the plaintiff is able to "pierce the corporate veil," he or she may recover against the officers, directors and shareholders even if there was no direct involvement in the deceptive practice.

Partners are jointly and severally liable for the actions of the other partners. Further, although the partners may have indemnification rights against each other, they are still jointly and severally liable to the consumer for damages.

STATUTES OF LIMITATION

In bringing a claim under a state consumer protection statute, one must determine the applicable statute of limitations period within which the claim must be initiated. The reader must consult the law of the jurisdiction in which the claim will be brought.

In general, the statute begins to run from the time a reasonable person would have discovered the facts constituting the deception. However, even if the consumer discovers the deception, if there is a false statement of a material fact which prevents the consumer from taking action, such as a promise to correct the problem, the statute may be extended.

PRECONDITIONS

Some state consumer protection statutes provide that certain conditions must be met before the consumer is permitted to file an action, such as mandatory settlement conferences.

In addition, some states require the consumer to have suffered damage before bringing an action, although the amount of damages suffered is irrelevant, and even minimal damages usually satisfy the statute.

Some states require the consumer to send the seller a notice or demand letter before filing a lawsuit. The purpose is to give the seller an opportunity to settle the matter so as to avoid clogging the courts with numerous consumer actions.

BANKRUPTCY

One who engages in unfair or deceptive practices may file for bankruptcy protection when faced with a claim under the state's consumer protection statute. Once a bankruptcy petition is filed, an automatic stay is issued by the court which suspends any actions pending against the bankrupt party.

If this should occur, the consumer should pursue his or her claim through the bankruptcy court by filing a proof of claim. A proof of claim may be filed whether or not the consumer's state claim has been filed, even if the precise amount of the claim cannot yet be determined. However, there is a time limit within which proofs of claim must be filed. Individual consumer claims are afforded a priority status under the Bankruptcy Code.

Under certain circumstances, the consumer may make a motion to the bankruptcy court to have the automatic stay lifted so that the consumer can proceed with his or her lawsuit against the bankrupt at the state level. This may occur when the bankrupt does not follow certain procedural requirements, such as getting a reorganization plan confirmed by the court.

JURISDICTION

Actions brought under state consumer protection statutes must follow the jurisdictional requirements of the state. Federal court jurisdiction may be obtained where the state claim is brought in conjunction with claims under federal laws, such as the Fair Debt Collection Practices Act, or the Truth-in-Lending Act.

Of course, as set forth above, if the seller declares bankruptcy, the federal bankruptcy court has jurisdiction over the claim unless the court lifts the automatic stay and permits the consumer to proceed with his or her claim at the state level.

CONSTITUTIONAL CONSIDERATIONS

Constitutional challenges to state consumer protection statutes usually do not prevail. The most widely used constitutional defense involves the First Amendment protection of the seller's speech. Although commercial speech may be protected, the Supreme Court has stated that false, deceptive or misleading advertising is not protected.

DAMAGES

A consumer brings an action under the state consumer protection statute seeking a remedy for the injuries that he or she suffered as a result of the seller's unfair or deceptive act or practice. If the statute did not provide a remedy, there would be little reason to spend one's time, energy and financial resources in bringing the claim.

A common remedy sought is a court-ordered injunction to prevent the seller from engaging in the prohibited conduct. The purpose of the injunction is to put the seller on notice that certain of their practices are prohibited, and to order the seller not to continue the prohibited practice. Other remedies include voiding or rescinding contracts, and monetary damage awards, as set forth below.

A successful consumer may be entitled to actual damages, such as out-of-pocket expenses or loss-of-bargain damages. Restitution is another available remedy. Pain and suffering may be awarded, however, where the consumer's claim is that of mental anguish, there may be certain additional requirements—e.g. physical manifestation of the mental anguish—depending on the jurisdiction.

Because attorney fees may be cost prohibitive in bringing a small consumer claim, some states have begun to award attorneys fees in addition to the monetary damage award to the consumer.

It is the consumer's responsibility to prove the damages and to demonstrate how those damages are related to the deception. Some states provide for minimum damage awards to plaintiff's who are able to prove that a violation has occurred. Multiple damage awards, e.g. treble damages, are available in some states provided that actual damages are proven. Further, where the seller's malice or reckless conduct is proven, punitive damages may be available in some jurisdictions.

CLASS ACTIONS

An effective method of deterring unfair and deceptive acts and practices by a particular seller is to join a number of small consumer claims into a class action. Procedures for bringing a consumer class action would be governed by the jurisdiction's class action statute unless the applicable consumer protection statute sets forth its own class action provisions.

DUTY OF GOOD FAITH AND FAIR DEALING

As set forth in the Restatement Second of the Law of Contracts, and further provided in the Uniform Commercial Code, every contract imposes upon each party a duty of good faith and fair dealing in its performance and its enforcement.

See Section 205 of the Restatement Second of the Law of Contracts set forth in the Appendix.

Good Faith

UCC Section 1-201(19) defines *good faith* as "honesty in fact in the conduct or transaction concerned." In the case of a merchant, the UCC Section 2-103(1)(b) provides that good faith means "honesty in fact and the observance of reasonable commercial standards of fair dealing in the trade."

The phrase "good faith" is used in a variety of contexts, and its meaning varies somewhat with the context. Good faith performance or enforcement of a contract emphasizes faithfulness to an agreed common purpose and consistency with the justified expectations of the other party.

It excludes a variety of types of conduct characterized as involving "bad faith" because they violate community standards of decency, fairness or reasonableness. The appropriate remedy for a breach of the duty of good faith also varies with the circumstances.

CHAPTER 8:
UNFAIR AND DECEPTIVE ACTS AND PRACTICES—LIABILITY AMONG SELLERS OF GOODS AND SERVICES

IN GENERAL

The Restatement Third of the Law of Unfair Competition sets forth the general law concerning protection of the commercial interests of sellers of goods and services from unfair competition and the deceptive acts and practices of other sellers.

Applicable sections of the Restatement Third of the Law of Unfair Competition are set forth at Appendix 4.

The use of unfair and deceptive representations in the marketing of goods and services may cause injury to the legitimate commercial interests of other sellers by unfairly depriving them of the opportunity to compete on the merits of their products in the marketplace, or by threatening harm to their reputation and good will.

Prohibited conduct includes making representations falsely describing the qualities or characteristics of a seller's goods or services, often referred to as "false advertising," and misrepresentations relating to the source of a seller's goods or services, sometimes referred to as "passing off."

Although the rules set forth in the Restatement are concerned with the protection of these commercial interests and are not applicable to actions by deceived purchasers, they function as an indirect form of consumer protection. A discussion of the law applicable to consumer complaints is set forth in this almanac.

HISTORICAL DEVELOPMENT

Liability to other sellers for commercial injuries resulting from an actor's deceptive marketing was initially confined to misrepresentations of source. Recognition of liability in the absence of a misrepresentation relating to source was inhibited by several factors:

(1) The seeming complexity of identifying appropriate plaintiffs;

(2) The fear that such liability might unduly hamper free enterprise;

(3) The development of alternative means of dealing with the problem of deceptive advertising; and

(4) The acceptance of precedents as exhaustive rather than illustrative.

During the first half of the 20th century, liability at common law was cautiously expanded beyond misrepresentations of source to misrepresentations concerning other characteristics or qualities of the seller's goods. However, courts generally required proof that the misrepresentation had directly diverted business from the plaintiff to the seller.

This requirement effectively precluded relief unless the plaintiff was the only other source of the misrepresented goods. This was known as the "single source" rule. This rule severely limited the capacity of the common law to respond to the problem of deceptive advertising. In addition, the Restatement of Torts retained the requirement of proof that the misrepresentation had diverted sales from the plaintiff to the seller.

Because the private right of act for false advertising was so limited, in the early decades of the twentieth century, many state legislatures enacted criminal prohibitions against false advertising. These statutes were referred to as the Printers Ink Statutes. However, these statutes also had little impact because they were subject to strict construction and sporadic enforcement.

The Federal Trade Commission Act, which prohibited "unfair methods of competition" and "unfair or deceptive acts or practices," established a comprehensive regulatory scheme dealing with deceptive advertising. However, there was no provision for private enforcement.

More recently, state legislatures, in large part due to the Federal Trade Commission's draft of the Unfair Trade Practices and Consumer Protection Act, began to enact "Little FTC Acts" to provide for public regulation at the state level.

Further, the private right of action by competitors for deceptive marketing was expanded with the enactment of the Trademark Act of 1946, commonly known as the Lanham Act. As originally enacted, § 43(a) recognized a right of action against "a false designation of origin, or any false description or representation" used in connection with any goods or services in favor of "any person who believes that he is or is likely to be damaged."

Some early interpretations confined § 43(a) of the Act to misrepresentations relating to source; other interpretations viewed it as a codification of existing common law liability under the "single source" doctrine. Subsequent decisions, however, established the section's general applicability to deceptive advertising.

The 1988 revision of § 43(a) of the Act clarified its application to both misrepresentations of source and other deceptive representations made in connection with the marketing of goods and services.

State legislation now also recognizes private rights of action in favor of businesses likely to be injured by deceptive marketing on the part of other sellers in the marketplace. A number of states have enacted the Uniform Deceptive Trade Practices Act, which is discussed further below.

DECEPTIVE MISREPRESENTATION

According to the Restatement, if one makes a representation in connection with the marketing of goods or services, relating to one's own goods, services, or commercial activities, that is likely to deceive or mislead prospective purchasers to the likely commercial detriment of another, he or she is subject to liability to the other. Again, this usually occurs through (1) false advertising; or (2) passing off.

False Advertising

False advertising refers to the prohibited practice by a seller of giving an untrue account of the qualities or characteristics of the seller's goods or services. Whether or not the representation is actionable depends on the factors set forth below.

Likelihood of Deception

In order to be liable, the representation must be likely to deceive or mislead "prospective purchasers." Prospective purchasers include any persons or legal entities to whom the seller's goods or services are marketed, whether by sale, lease, license, or other manner of commercial transaction, or to whom an offer of such a transaction is made.

The likelihood that a particular representation will deceive or mislead is determined by the meaning likely to be attributed to the representation by the purchaser, and the relationship between that meaning and the true facts. A representation may be likely to deceive or mislead because it is literally false, such as a claim that a piece of jewelry is solid gold when it is only gold plated.

Representations that are not literally false may nevertheless be likely to deceive or mislead if the purchaser is likely to infer additional facts that are false. Thus, a statement may be true with respect to the facts stated but fail to include additional information necessary to prevent the implication of additional false assertions. These half-truths may be as likely to deceive or mislead as a literally false representation. This reasoning would also apply to an ambiguous statement which is subject to two interpretations, one of which is false.

When the representation is literally false, a court may conclude that the representation is likely to deceive or mislead. However, when the tendency to deceive or mislead is instead based upon the inferences which may be drawn, or upon a choice among several possible interpretations, direct evidence of the meaning attached to the representation by the purchaser may be necessary to establish a likelihood of deception.

Further, evidence of actual deception, misunderstanding, or confusion, although not required under the Restatement Third of the Law of Unfair Competition, is relevant in determining whether the purchaser is likely to be deceived or misled.

In addition, the intentions of the speaker are also relevant in assessing the likelihood of deception, although intent is not required to assess liability. Nevertheless, evidence that the speaker intended to communicate a false or misleading message may justify the inference that deception is likely.

In many instances a representation may be likely to deceive or mislead only some of the prospective purchasers to whom it is directed. However, under the Restatement, a person is subject to liability only if the representation is likely to deceive or mislead a significant portion of the prospective purchasers as a whole. Nevertheless, if the representation would deceive a reasonably prudent purchaser, that will usually suffice.

On the other hand, if a reasonably prudent purchaser would not be deceived or misled by the representation, the seller would probably not be liable unless further evidence indicates that the representation is nevertheless likely to deceive or mislead a significant portion of purchasers as a whole.

Intent Irrelevant

Liability under this section of the Restatement concerns an objective evaluation of the probable consequences of the seller's conduct, and not upon his or her subjective intent. Although intent may be relevant to some issues, such as the meaning to be attributed to the words or conduct of the seller, an intent to deceive is not a necessary element of liability. The history of the law of unfair competition reveals a persistent retreat from its emphasis on state of mind.

Statutory actions for unfair competition have similarly abandoned the requirement of fraudulent intent. Liability for deceptive marketing under §43(a) of the Lanham Act is not dependent on the defendant's intent. Under the Uniform Deceptive Trade Practices Act, a person causing confusion as to source, sponsorship, or affiliation, or falsely describing the characteristics, ingredients, or benefits of the goods or services, is similarly subject to liability without regard to intent. In keeping with the trend of common law developments and the prevailing statutory formulations, the rule under the Restatement does not require proof of fraudulent intent.

The Manner of Misrepresentation

There are no technical requirements as to the manner in which the misrepresentation must be made for liability to attach. It may be conveyed at the point of sale on packaging or displays, or it may be contained in brochures and catalogs, or in print, radio, or television advertising. The misrepresentation may be written or oral, and may even be conveyed through visual images

Commercial Detriment

The fact that a seller has made a representation that is likely to deceive or mislead is not in itself sufficient to subject the seller to liability. Liability may be imposed under the Restatement only if the deception is likely to cause harm to the commercial interests of the other.

A representation is likely to harm the commercial interests of another if:

1. The representation is material, in that it is likely to affect the conduct of prospective purchasers; and

2. There is a reasonable basis for believing that the representation has caused or is likely to cause a diversion of trade from the other or harm to the other's reputation or good will.

Materiality

The materiality of a representation, like its meaning, must be determined from the perspective of the prospective purchasers to whom it is directed. The representation need not be the sole or predominant factor influencing the conduct of the prospective purchasers. If a significant number of prospective purchasers are likely to attach importance to the representation in determining whether to engage in a proposed transaction, the representation is considered material.

Evidence indicating an intent to deceive, however, may justify an inference that the representation is material since a seller will not ordinarily make a fraudulent representation without believing that the representation is likely to influence prospective purchasers.

If a representation is not likely to be relied upon by prospective purchasers, it is not a material representation. Further, if the falsity of the representation is so obvious that it is unlikely any prospective purchasers would rely on it, it would not be considered material.

Material representations commonly take the form of statements that pertain directly to the quality or characteristics of the seller's goods or services, however, a representation that indirectly relates to the product's quality may also be material. Representations that concern matters that are of little or no significance to prospective purchasers would not be considered material.

The propensity of sellers to exaggerate the advantages of goods or services—also known as "puffing"—is well known, and to some extent buyers are expected to and do understand that they should not place their full faith in such self-serving statements. Therefore, general statements of praise, without reference to specific facts, are unlikely to affect the conduct of prospective purchasers and would not be considered material.

Likelihood of Harm

In order to subject the seller to liability, the misrepresentation must be likely to cause harm to the commercial interests of the person seeking relief. Proof that such harm has actually occurred is not necessary. The seller is subject to liability if the evidence indicates that there is a reasonable probability that the person seeking relief has or will suffer harm as a result of the misrepresentation.

Imposition of liability according to this rule serves as an indirect form of consumer protection. Thus, when the potential injury to deceived consumers is relatively great, a more modest likelihood of harm to competitors may be sufficient to subject the seller to liability.

Commercial Detriment

Commercial detriment sufficient to subject a seller to liability may also be found in a threat of harm to the business reputation or good will of another. In determining the existence of likely commercial detriment, the issue is whether the party seeking relief has a reasonable interest to be protected against the deceptive marketing of the other.

Remedies

Injunctive Relief

For injunctive relief to be granted, proof of actual deception or actual harm is not required provided there is a showing that the misrepresentation is likely to deceive or mislead prospective purchasers to the likely commercial detriment of the party seeking relief. Further, injunctive relief may be awarded even though the fact or extent of harm is uncertain. Such a remedy does not afford a windfall to the plaintiff and furthers the public interest in preserving the integrity of the marketplace.

Monetary Relief

A person seeking monetary relief bears the additional burden of establishing entitlement to such relief under the rules stated in Sections 36 and 37 of the Restatement. Those rules generally require proof of actual deception resulting in demonstrable pecuniary loss to the plaintiff or demonstrable pecuniary gain to the defendant.

See Sections 36 and 37 of the Restatement Third of the Law of Unfair Competition set forth at Appendix 4.

Passing Off

Passing off refers to the prohibited practice by a seller of misrepresenting the source of the seller's goods or services. The term passing off refers to any situation in which the seller's conduct creates a likelihood that prospective purchasers will be confused concerning the source of the goods or services. Intent is irrelevant.

See Section 4 of the Restatement Third of the Law of Unfair Competition set forth at Appendix 4.

If the person falsely connected with the seller, or with the seller's goods or services, is in competition with the seller, reliance on the misrepresentation by prospective purchasers may divert business from that person to the seller. If the purchaser is subsequently dissatisfied with the seller's goods or services, this may also result in harm to the innocent party's reputation and good will. Thus, this provision affords protection against both diversion of business, and harm to reputation and good will.

Likelihood of Deception

In order to subject the seller to liability, the representation must create a likelihood that a significant portion of the prospective purchasers as a whole will be deceived or misled with respect to the identity of the seller, or the source of the seller's goods or services.

Again, proof of actual deception is not required. The issuance of an injunction upon proof that deception is likely to protect both the expectations of consumers, and the innocent party from harm that may be impossible to quantify for purposes of monetary relief.

Complainants seeking a monetary recovery, however, must also establish entitlement to such relief, which generally require proof of actual deception resulting in demonstrable pecuniary loss to the complainant or demonstrable pecuniary gain to the seller.

Although an intent to deceive is not an element of the cause of action, evidence that the representation was in fact intended to mislead prospective purchasers with respect to the identity of the seller, or the source of the goods or services, may justify an inference that deception is likely. If so, the burden may shift to the seller to demonstrate that deception is unlikely. Again, the subjective intent of the seller is relevant to an award of monetary relief.

A misrepresentation of source can be made in any manner sufficient to communicate the misrepresentation to prospective purchasers. Thus, the misrepresentation may appear on packaging, or it may be communicated through advertising or by assertions made at the point of sale. The misrepresentation may also be implied from the seller's conduct.

Reverse Passing Off

According to the Restatement, the seller is also subject to liability if, in marketing goods or services manufactured, produced, or supplied by the another, the seller makes a representation likely to deceive or mislead prospective purchasers by causing the mistaken belief that the seller or a third person is the manufacturer, producer, or supplier of the goods or services, if the representation is to the likely commercial detriment of the other.

See Section 5 of the Restatement Third of the Law of Unfair Competition at Appendix 4.

This form of misrepresentation is referred to as reverse passing off. The misrepresentations of source that are the subject of reverse passing off differ from traditional passing off in that they result in the passing off of another's goods as those of the seller, rather than the passing of the seller's goods as those of another.

Although all forms of passing off involve the creation of confusion with respect to the source of goods or services, the threat of harm to the commercial interests of others is less immediate in the case of reverse passing off.

Reverse passing off does not directly threaten the reputation of another because the misrepresentation cuts of the actual party's association with the goods or services marketed by the seller. Similarly, it cannot be said that the actual party is subject to a direct diversion of business in the usual sense since the goods have already been sold.

Reverse passing off, however, may sometimes misrepresent the relative capabilities or accomplishments of the parties, thus creating the likelihood of a future diversion of business to the seller. If the actual party can establish both the fact of a misrepresentation and a likelihood of harm to its commercial relations, the seller may be liable.

Likelihood of Deception

A misrepresentation involving reverse passing off can be actionable if it is likely to deceive or mislead a significant portion of prospective purchasers as a whole. Again, proof of an intent to deceive or actual deception is not required. The seller's representation may be expressed in words or implied by other conduct, but the complainant bears the burden of proving that deception is likely.

Proof that the seller has removed the trade name of the original party and replaced it with its own name does not in itself establish a likelihood of deception. The circumstances must indicate that prospective purchasers are likely to view the presence of the seller's name as a representation that the seller is the manufacturer, producer, or supplier, and not simply a marketer of the goods.

In the absence of an express or implied misrepresentation relating to source, the sale of goods from which the manufacturer's name has been removed or replaced by the seller's name amounts to mere non-disclosure for which the seller is not subject to liability.

Commercial Detriment.

In traditional passing off, the misrepresentation of source ordinarily threatens a diversion of business, or harm to reputation and good will, and is thus to the likely commercial detriment of the person falsely represented as the source of the goods or services.

The misrepresentations that are the subject of reverse passing off, however, are not as clearly harmful to the interests of the other. Therefore, the complainant bears the burden of proving that harm to its commercial relations is in fact likely.

It may be that prospective purchasers simply do not care about the physical source of the goods or services, but rather choose to rely on the reputation or expertise of the seller. In that case, such a misrepresentation would not be material, thus, the seller would not be liable. Further, the seller would not be liable if the manufacturer expressly or implicitly consented to sales under the seller's trade name.

Misrepresentations in Marketing the Goods or Services of Another

According to the Restatement, one is subject to liability to another if, in marketing goods or services of which the other is truthfully identified as the manufacturer, producer, or supplier, the seller makes a representation relating to those goods or services that is likely to deceive or mislead prospective purchasers to the likely commercial detriment of the other.

See Section 6 of the Restatement Third of the Law of Unfair Competition set forth at Appendix 4.

This rule applies to situations in which the representation relates to goods or services truthfully identified as originating from another.

Liability for the misrepresentations that are within the scope of this section has long been recognized as actionable at common law, and liability has also been imposed under §43(a) of the Lanham Act and other statutes, including the Uniform Deceptive Trade Practices Act.

Under this section, the misrepresentation may be express or implied, and proof of actual deception or of an intention to deceive is not required. The misrepresentations are typically made in an attempt to sell goods that the actor has on hand, and are thus generally laudatory rather than derogatory.

A seller may assert, for example, that the goods are fresh when in fact they are stale, or that manufacturer's seconds are of the highest quality.

However, if the misrepresentation is derogatory, as is the case in "bait and switch" advertising, the actor may also be subject to liability for product disparagement, as set forth below.

Although proof of actual harm is not required, the original manufacturer, producer, or supplier of the goods or services bears the burden of proving that the misrepresentation is to its likely commercial detriment. Again, commercial detriment to the person identified as the source of the goods or services is likely if the misrepresentation threatens to divert business from that person to the seller.

A misrepresentation is also to the likely commercial detriment of the manufacturer or supplier if it is likely to diminish the reputation of the goods in the eyes of prospective purchasers.

CONTRIBUTORY LIABILITY

According to the Restatement, other parties may be contributorily liable for their part in the deceptive representations, as set forth below.

See Sections 7 and 8 of the Restatement Third of the Law of Unfair Competition set forth at Appendix 4.

Contributory Liability of Printers, Publishers and Other Suppliers

The rule states that one who, by supplying materials or rendering services to a third person, directly and substantially assists the third person in making a representation that subjects the third person to liability to another for deceptive marketing is subject to liability to that other for contributory deceptive marketing.

However, if the party subject to contributory liability acted without knowledge that he or she was assisting the third person in making a representation likely to deceive or mislead, injunctive relief would be the only appropriate remedy available to the aggrieved party.

This provision subjects to liability those who directly and substantially assist another in misrepresenting goods or services, such as persons who design or supply materials communicating the misrepresentation —e.g. the packaging and advertisements —and those who disseminate the misrepresentation by publication or broadcast.

Liability under this Section does not extend to those who supply basic materials or services only incidentally related to the misrepresentation.

Contributory Liability of Manufacturers and Distributors

Under this rule, one who markets goods or services to a third person who further markets the goods or services in a manner that subjects the third person to liability to another for deceptive marketing is subject to liability to that other for contributory deceptive marketing if:

1. It intentionally induces the third person to engage in such conduct; or

2. It fails to take reasonable precautions against the occurrence of the third person's conduct in circumstances in which that conduct can be reasonably anticipated.

Further, if a manufacturer or distributor seeks to further its economic interests by inducing others to market its goods or services in a proscribed manner, it is subject to liability under this Section.

THE UNIFORM DECEPTIVE TRADE PRACTICES ACT

The Uniform Deceptive Trade Practices Act (UDTPA) was promulgated by the National Conference of Commissioners on Uniform State Laws in 1964 and revised in 1966. The Prefatory Note to the 1964 Act states the purpose of the Act as follows:

> The Uniform Act is designed to bring state law up to date by removing undue restrictions on the common law action for deceptive trade practices. Certain objectionable practices are singled out, but the courts are left free to fix the proper ambit of the Act in case-by-case adjudications. The deceptive trade practices singled out by the Uniform Act can be roughly subdivided into conduct involving either misleading trade identification or false or deceptive advertising.

Thus, the purpose of the UDTPA is to afford prospective purchasers the ability to compare products offered by competing sellers. Without this ability, the free enterprise system cannot operate efficiently because the use of deceptive representations in the marketing of goods and services impairs the ability of purchasers to make informed and intelligent choices. In addition, as confidence in the truth of advertising diminishes, prospective purchasers may be forced to expend additional funds in inspecting the competing products.

A seller's misrepresentations may be actionable by deceived purchasers under traditional rules of tort and contract law and also under the various state and federal consumer protection statutes. Unfortunately, the expenses of obtaining such relief may be cost prohibitive to the consumer.

Among the practices proscribed by the UDTPA are deceptive designations of geographic origin; representations that the goods or services have characteristics, ingredients, uses, benefits, or quantities that they do not in fact possess; and false representations that goods are original or new, or are of a particular standard, quality, or grade.

Injunctions may be granted under the Uniform Deceptive Trade Practices Act to persons likely to be damaged by the deceptive practice. In addition, in several states, either by express statutory authorization or judicial interpretation, competitors damaged by deceptive practices may also bring private actions under the Unfair Trade Practices and Consumer Protection Act.

The state statutes governing unfair and deceptive acts and practices are set forth at Appendix 3.

PRODUCT DISPARAGEMENT

According to the Restatement, to be actionable, a representation disparaging a product must relate to the goods, services, or commercial activities of the seller. The general rules governing product disparagement, or "trade libel" as it is sometimes called, are set forth in Restatement Second of the Law of Torts.

Under the 1988 revision of §43(a) of the Lanham Act, and under §2(a)(8) of the Uniform Deceptive Trade Practices Act, one who falsely disparages the goods or services of another seller is subject to liability without proof of special damages or of an intent to deceive, thus diminishing the distinctions drawn at common law between disparagement and false advertising.

FIRST AMENDMENT CONSIDERATIONS

The United States Supreme Court has held that the first amendment protects communications promoting the sale of goods or services from unjustified governmental interference, but it has repeatedly affirmed that there is no constitutional prohibition on the imposition of liability in connection with false, deceptive, or misleading commercial speech.

CHAPTER 9:
TRUTH IN LENDING

IN GENERAL

A consumer has the right to obtain complete and accurate information concerning a particular transaction before making a final decision. Sellers and creditors are obligated under state and federal laws to provide the consumer with this information.

For example, manufacturers of food products are required to include certain information on the packaging of their products, such as the nutritional value, ingredients and weight, etc. Creditors, including grantors of retail installment loans, are required to disclose all of the relevant terms of the credit transaction.

In 1968, Congress enacted the Truth in Lending Act. The purpose of the Act is ". . . to assure a meaningful disclosure of credit terms so that the consumer will be able to compare more readily the various credit terms available to him. . . " The Act preempts any state laws which are inconsistent with its disclosure provisions. Regulation "Z" refers to the regulations of the Federal Reserve Board which implement the provisions of the Act.

The Act pertains to "creditors," who are defined as persons:

(1) who regularly extend . . . consumer credit which is payable by agreement in more than four installments, or for which the payment of a finance charge is or may be required; and

(2) to whom the debt arising from the consumer credit transaction is initially payable on the face of the indebtedness, or by agreement.

DISCLOSURE REQUIREMENTS

Under the Act, creditors are required to disclose relevant information concerning credit transactions. Disclosure must be made in writing and in a clear and conspicuous manner. In addition, the disclosures must be made in a timely manner so as to give the consumer a chance to consider them fully before entering into the transaction.

The most important disclosure requirement of the Act relates to finance charges. The finance charge is defined as "the sum of all charges payable directly or indirectly by the person to whom the credit is extended and imposed directly or indirectly by the creditor as an incident to the extension of credit." This would include such items as interest; service charges; loan fees; insurance premiums; or other similar fees.

The Act also imposes disclosure requirements in connection with soliciting business through advertising. For example, creditors may not advertise any specific terms unless they will actually be available to the consumer.

REMEDIES

If a creditor violates the Act, it is liable to the consumer for actual damages. For example, an understatement of the finance charge will result in actual damages to the consumer of the difference between the finance charge as stated, and the finance charge as actually assessed. Nevertheless, if actual damages are not present, violations of the Act still result in liability as set forth in the statute. Further, a successful consumer plaintiff is generally entitled to legal fees expended in enforcing the statute.

CHAPTER 10:
FAIR CREDIT REPORTING

IN GENERAL

When a consumer applies for credit, such as a credit card, an automobile loan, etc., he or she generally fills out an application form which sets forth information concerning the consumer's creditworthiness. In considering the application, the creditor generally requests a report from a credit reporting agency to verify the information, and to obtain additional information concerning the consumer's ability to take on additional debt, and his or her credit payment history, e.g. whether the consumer is a late or timely payor.

All major credit granters routinely supply credit reporting agencies information concerning the payment history of its customers. The credit reporting agency also searches public records to determine whether the consumer has any judgments or liens filed which would affect their creditworthiness.

OBLIGATION TO MAINTAIN ACCURATE, CONFIDENTIAL AND CURRENT INFORMATION

This information is helpful to both creditor and consumer provided it is (1) accurate, and (2) maintained in a manner so as to protect the applicant's privacy rights. For example, the consumer must authorize the creditor to obtain his or her credit report. Unauthorized release of this information may result in an action for invasion of the consumer's right to privacy. In addition, inaccurate information, such as reporting the consumer as a late payor, may result in a defamation action. Nevertheless, both of these remedies have their shortcomings when applied to consumer actions.

In response to the inadequacy of these remedies, Congress enacted the Fair Credit Reporting Act (FCRA) in 1970 as part of its Consumer Credit Protection Act. The FCRA preempts any state statutes which are inconsistent with its provisions.

Under the FCRA, creditors—defined as "users"—can only obtain a consumer's credit report for limited purposes, the most common of which are extension of credit or employment.

In addition, a creditor may only request a credit report for the individual consumer involved in the transaction, and cannot obtain a spouse's credit report if the spouse is not a party to the transaction. It is a crime under the FCRA to obtain a consumer's credit report under false pretenses.

If the credit reporting agency willfully or negligently issues a report to a person who does not have a permissible purpose in obtaining the report, the agency is subject to civil liability, and an individual employee who knowingly and willingly issues the report may be subject to criminal sanctions.

The credit reporting agencies are also required to maintain accurate information, and to permit consumers to correct any inaccuracies found in their reports. The agency is not subject to civil liability for inaccuracies contained in consumer credit reports provided they "follow reasonable procedures to assure maximum possible accuracy of the information..."

However, if the agency does not follow reasonable procedures, they may be subject to liability. If the consumer disputes the accuracy of information contained in his or her file, the agency is required to reinvestigate this information within a reasonable period of time.

If, upon reinvestigation, the information cannot be verified, or is proved inaccurate, it must be deleted, and corrected copies must be sent to all parties who had recently requested copies of the report. However, if the agency believes upon reinvestigation that the information is accurate, the consumer is entitled to include a statement of dispute in the report.

TIME LIMITATIONS

Credit reporting agencies are also required to make sure the information contained in the consumer's file is current. The rationale for this requirement is to give the consumer a chance to rehabilitate a negative credit history. In general, negative information, such as delinquent accounts, judgments, liens, or charge-offs, must be deleted after seven years.

The seven year period starts to run from the date of the negative activity. For example, a delinquent account may be reported as delinquent for seven years from the date it becomes delinquent. If the delinquency subsequently becomes a charge-off, it may be reported as a charge-off for seven years from that date.

There are certain exceptions to, and extensions of, the seven-year rule, so the reader is advised to check the statute. The most common exception involves bankruptcy cases, which may be reported for ten years.

REMEDIES

A credit reporting agency or user is liable to the consumer for any actual damages suffered as a result of negligence. Actual damages generally include monetary losses and have also been held to include damages for mental anguish resulting from aggravation, embarrassment, humiliation and injury to reputation, etc. Further, if the violation is willful, punitive damages may also be available to the consumer.

CHAPTER 11:
THE FAIR DEBT COLLECTION PRACTICES ACT

IN GENERAL

If a consumer defaults in his or her payment obligation, the creditor will likely undertake some sort of debt collection. The first attempts to collect the debt are usually of a nonjudicial nature, either by the internal collection department of the creditor, or by an independent collection agency with whom the creditor contracts.

Initial contacts are often by letter or telephone. Absent success, some debt collectors take increasingly invasive measures to attempt to collect the debt. If the creditor is unable to collect the debt voluntarily from the consumer, the creditor's remedy is usually limited to litigation to acquire a judgment against the consumer.

This chapter is concerned with the debt collection procedures prior to the litigation stage. Under the common law, there exist a number of theories under which an aggrieved consumer can retaliate against unfair debt collection procedures. These theories include, but are not limited to, intentional infliction of emotional distress, defamation, and invasion of the right to privacy.

Almost all jurisdictions have enacted some sort of statute pertaining to fair debt collection, many of which are patterned after the Fair Debt Collection Practices Act. In addition, the consumer may find remedies in Section 5 of the Federal Trade Commission Act which deals with unfair or deceptive acts or practices in connection with debt collection.

In 1988, the Fair Debt Collection Practices Act (FDCPA) was enacted to supplement the available statutory and common law tort remedies available to the consumer to restrain unfair debt collection procedures. The FDCPA contains detailed provisions regulating the manner in which debt collection is carried out. However, the FDCPA applies only to debt collection agencies whereas the state statutes modeled after the FDCPA generally apply to creditors as well.

OBLIGATIONS OF DEBT COLLECTORS UNDER THE FDCPA

The FDCPA requires debt collectors to provide information about the alleged debt, and verification of the debt, at the request of the consumer, including the name of the creditor, the amount of the debt, and an offer to provide the name of the original creditor, if different.

In addition, a statement must be sent, generally with the first communication between debt collector and consumer, basically advising the consumer that the debt will be assumed valid if the consumer fails to dispute its validity within 30 days, and that any dispute will result in verification of the debt to the consumer by the collector.

PROHIBITED PRACTICES UNDER THE FDCPA

The FDCPA prohibits various kinds of collection practices, including, but not limited to:

1. Communicating with the consumer at an unusual or inconvenient time or place;

2. Communicating with the consumer at his or her place of employment if the employer prohibits such communications, or if the consumer requests that he or she not be contacted there;

3. Communicating with a consumer who is represented by an attorney;

4. Communicating with third parties without the authorization of the consumer;

5. Communicating with the consumer after he or she has notified the debt collector that there be no further communication concerning the debt. In this case, the debt collector may not contact the consumer except for the limited purpose of advising the consumer, in writing, of further action to be taken;

6. Making false, deceptive or misleading representations;

7. Using unfair or unconscionable conduct to collect the debt; and

8. Using harassing, threatening or otherwise abusive conduct to collect the debt.

REMEDIES

If a debt collector violates any of the provisions of the FDCPA, he or she is liable to the person with whom the violation took place. This would include the debtor and any other persons who were subject to the debt collector's improper tactics. The statute of limitations on bringing an action under the FDCPA is one year.

The consumer is entitled to actual damages, including physical or emotional injury, and actual expenses. The consumer is also entitled to statutory damages as set forth in the Act, whether or not actual damages exist, and whether or not the violation was intentional or inadvertent. Consumers who prevail on their claim may also be entitled to legal fees and costs at the discretion of the court.

CHAPTER 12: THE MAIL OR TELEPHONE ORDER MERCHANDISE RULE

OVERVIEW

The Mail or Telephone Order Merchandise Rule applies to most goods a customer orders from the seller by mail, telephone, fax, or on the Internet. It does not matter how the merchandise is advertised, how the customer pays, or who initiates the contact. The Rule requires that when a seller advertises merchandise, the seller must have a reasonable basis for stating or implying that they can ship within a certain time. If the seller makes no shipment statement, they must have a reasonable basis for believing that they can ship within 30 days. That is why direct marketers sometimes call this the "30-day Rule."

If, after taking the customer's order, the seller learns that they cannot ship within the time stated or within 30 days, they must seek the customer's consent to the delayed shipment. If the seller cannot obtain the customer's consent to the delay—either because it is not a situation in which you are permitted to treat the customer's silence as consent and the customer has not expressly consented to the delay, or because the customer has expressly refused to consent—the seller must, without being asked, promptly refund all the money the customer paid for the unshipped merchandise.

The text of The Mail or Telephone Order Merchandise Rule is set forth at Appendix 5.

REASONABLE BASIS

When a seller offers to sell merchandise, they must have a "reasonable basis" for:

1. Any express or implied shipment representation, or

2. Believing they can ship within 30 days of receipt of an order if they make no shipment representation or if the shipment representation is not clear and conspicuous.

Whenever the seller changes the shipment date by providing a delay notice, the seller must have a "reasonable basis" for:

1. The new shipment date, or

2. Any representation that they do not know when they can ship the merchandise.

When the seller takes orders by telephone, they may choose to provide prospective customers with updated shipment information. This may differ from what the seller said or implied about the shipment time in their advertising. The updated shipment information the seller provides on the telephone supersedes any shipment representation they made in the advertising. The seller also must have a reasonable basis for the updated shipment representation.

"Reasonable basis" means that the merchant has, at the time of making the representation, such information as would under the circumstances satisfy a reasonable and prudent businessperson, acting in good faith, that the representation is true. The evidence the seller needs to demonstrate the reasonableness of their shipment representations varies with circumstances. The following, however, is important:

Anticipated demand. Is the demand for each advertised item reasonably anticipated?

1. Supply. For each advertised item, is there a sufficient inventory on hand or adequate sources of supply to meet the anticipated demand for the product?

2. Fulfillment system. For all promotions in the relevant sales seasons, can the fulfillment system handle the cumulative anticipated demand for all products?

3. Recordkeeping. Are adequate records kept of the key events in each individual transaction to ensure that items can be shipped within the applicable time, as established by the Rule?

SALES INVOLVING CREDIT APPLICATIONS

If a customer applies to establish an in-house new credit account or increase an existing credit line to pay for the merchandise they order, the Rule provides the following:

1. If the seller makes no shipment representation when they solicit the order, they are allowed 50 (instead of 30) days to ship the order. The extra 20 days is to enable the seller to process the credit application. If they wish to use this provision of the Rule, they must have a reasonable basis to believe they can ship in 50 days.

2. If the seller does make a shipment representation when they solicit the order, they must have a reasonable basis for being able to ship in that time, regardless of whether the order is accompanied by an application for credit or extension of a credit line. The seller is presumed to have factored in the time needed to process the credit application or to have qualified the shipment representation appropriately.

OBLIGATION TO SHIP

The obligation to ship or take other action under the Rule begins as soon as the seller receives a "properly completed" order. An order is properly completed when the seller receives the correct full or partial payment, accompanied by all the information the seller needs to fill the order. Payment may be by cash, check, money order, the customer's authorization to charge an existing account, the customer's application for credit to pay for the order, or any substitute for these transactions that the seller accepts.

It is irrelevant when the seller posts or deposits payment, when checks clear, or when the seller's bank credits their account. The clock begins to run when the seller receives a properly completed order. However, if a customer's check is returned or a customer is refused credit, the Rule stops the shipment clock. It is reset at day one when the customer gives the seller cash, the customer's check is honored, or the seller receives notice that the customer qualifies for credit. At this point, the seller may take the amount of time originally stated to fulfill the order.

DELAY IN SHIPMENT

If a seller finds that they cannot ship on time, the seller must decide whether they will ever be able to ship the order. If the seller decides that they cannot, the seller must promptly cancel the order and make a full refund. If the seller decides they can ship the order later, the seller must seek the customer's consent to the delay. The seller may use whatever means they wish to obtain consent—such as the telephone, fax, mail, or email—as long as they notify the customer of the delay reasonably quickly. The customer must have sufficient advance notification to make a meaningful decision to consent to the delay or cancel the order.

Some businesses adopt internal deadlines that are earlier than those set by the Rule to ensure that their delay notices give all customers a meaningful opportunity to consent to the delay. If businesses fail to ship or give delay notifications by their internal deadlines, they automatically cancel the orders and make refunds.

In any event, no notification to the customer can take longer than the time originally promised or, if no time was promised, 30 days. If the seller cannot ship the order or provide the notice within this time, they must cancel the order and make a prompt refund.

First Delay Option Notice

In seeking a customer's consent to delay, the first delay notice the seller provides to the customer (the "delay option" notice) must include:

1. A definite revised shipment date or, if unknown, a statement that the seller is unable to provide a revised shipment date;

2. A statement that, if the customer chooses not to wait, the customer can cancel the order and obtain a full and prompt refund; and

3. Some means for the customer to choose to cancel at the seller's expense (e.g., by providing a postage prepaid reply card or toll-free telephone number).

The following information must be included when the seller cannot provide a revised shipping date:

1. The reason for the delay, and

2. A statement that, if the customer agrees to the indefinite delay, the customer may cancel the order any time until the seller ships the merchandise.

If the seller's first delay option notice provides a definite revised shipping date of 30 days or less, the seller must inform customers that their non-response will be treated as a consent to the delay.

A sample seller's first delay option notice (30 Days or Less) is set forth at Appendix 6.

If the seller's first delay option notice provides a definite revised shipping date of more than 30 days or states that they do not know when they will be able to ship, the seller must tell the customers that if they do not respond, the order will be cancelled automatically within the originally promised time plus 30 days.

A sample seller's first delay option notice (Indefinite or 30 Days or More) is set forth at Appendix 7.

Renewed Delay Option Notices

If the seller cannot ship the merchandise by the definite revised shipment date included in their most recent delay option notice, before that date they must seek the consent of their customers to any further delay. The seller must do this by providing customers a "renewed" delay option notice. A renewed delay option notice is similar in many ways to the first delay option notice. One important difference is that the customer's silence may not be treated as a consent to delay.

A renewed delay option notice must include:

1. A definite revised shipment date or, if unknown, a statement that the seller is unable to provide any date;

2. A statement that, if the customer chooses not to wait, the customer can cancel the order immediately and obtain a full and prompt refund;

3. A statement that, unless the seller receives notice that the customer agrees to wait beyond the most recent definite revised shipment date and the seller has not shipped by then, the customer's order automatically will be cancelled and a prompt refund will be provided; and

4. Some means for the customer to inform the seller at the seller's expense (e.g., by providing a postage prepaid reply card or toll-free telephone number) whether the customer agrees to the delay or is canceling the order.

The following information must be included when the seller cannot provide a new definite revised shipping date:

1. The reason for the delay, and

2. A statement that, if the customer agrees to the indefinite delay, the customer may cancel the order any time until the merchandise is shipped.

If the seller has provided an appropriate and timely delay option notice and the customer agrees to an indefinite revised shipment date, no additional delay notices are required.

CANCELLATION

Instead of seeking the customer's consent to delay, a seller can always cancel the order and send a refund. In that case, the seller must notify the customer and send the refund within the time they would have sent any delay notice required by the Rule.

The seller must cancel an order and provide a prompt refund when:

1. The customer exercises any option to cancel before the merchandise is shipped;

2. The customer does not respond to the seller's first notice of a definite revised shipment date of 30 days or less and the seller has not shipped the merchandise or received the customer's consent to a further delay by the definite revised shipment date;

3. The customer does not respond to the seller's notice of a definite revised shipment date of more than 30 days (or the seller's notice that they are unable to provide a definite revised shipment date) and the seller has not shipped the merchandise within 30 days of the original shipment date;

4. The customer consents to a definite delay and the seller has not shipped or obtained the customer's consent to any additional delay by the shipment time the customer consented to;

5. The seller has not shipped or provided the required delay or renewed option notices on time; or

6. The seller determines that they will never be able to ship the merchandise.

REFUNDS

When the seller must make a Rule-required refund, the following applies:

1. If the customer paid by cash, check, or money order, you must refund the correct amount by first class mail within seven working days after the order is cancelled.

2. If the customer paid by credit, you must credit the customer's account or notify the customer that the account will not be charged, within one customer's billing cycle, after the order is cancelled.

If the seller cannot ship any of the merchandise ordered by the customer, they must refund the entire amount the customer "tendered," including any shipping, handling, insurance, or other costs. If the seller ships some, but not all, of the merchandise ordered, they must refund the difference between the total amount paid and the amount the customer would have paid, according to their ordering instructions, for the shipped items only.

When making Rule-required refunds, the seller cannot substitute credit toward future purchases, credit vouchers, or scrip. When the order is paid for in whole or in part by proofs of purchase, coupons, or other promotional devices, the seller must provide "reasonable compensation" to the customer for the proofs of purchase plus any shipping, handling, or other charges the customer paid.

RECORDKEEPING

Although the Rule does not require the seller to keep records, an accurate, up-to-date recordkeeping system can help show that the seller is complying with the Rule. This is especially important because, in any action to enforce the Rule, if the seller cannot document their use of systems and procedures for complying, the Rule provides that the seller bears the burden of proving they do comply. Documentation should address the following:

1. Substantiation for shipment representations.

2. Fulfillment system.

3. Order recordkeeping.

In addition, if the seller provides delay option notices by telephone, they may want to keep accurate records of the scripts used.

Records should be kept for at least as long as the applicable statute of limitations applies. The statute of limitations on actions to enforce the Rule is three years for consumer redress and five years for civil penalties. State statutes of limitations for individual customer or state actions are sometimes longer. The reader is advised to check the law of their own jurisdiction for specific provisions.

EXCEPTIONS TO RULE

The following sales are exempt from the Rule:

1. Magazine subscriptions (and similar serial deliveries), except for the first shipment;

2. Sales of seeds and growing plants;

3. Orders made on a collect-on-delivery basis (C.O.D.); and,

4. Transactions covered by the FTC's Negative Option Rule (such as book and music clubs).

5. Services, such as mail order photo-finishing.

PENALTIES

Merchants who violate the Rule can be sued by the FTC for injunctive relief, monetary civil penalties of up to $11,000 per violation (any time during the five years preceding the filing of the complaint), and consumer redress (any time during the three years preceding the filing of the complaint). When the mails are involved, the Postal Service also has authority to take action for problems such as non-delivery. State law enforcement agencies can take action for violating state consumer protection laws.

UNORDERED MERCHANDISE

Whether or not the Rule is involved, in any approval or other sale, the seller must obtain the customer's prior express agreement to receive the merchandise. Otherwise the merchandise may be treated as unordered merchandise. It is unlawful to:

1. Send any merchandise *by any means* without the express request of the recipient (unless the merchandise is clearly identified as a gift, free sample, or the like); or,

2. Try to obtain payment for or the return of the unordered merchandise.

Merchants who ship unordered merchandise with knowledge that it is unlawful to do so can be subject to civil penalties of up to $11,000 per violation. Moreover, customers who receive unordered merchandise are legally entitled to treat the merchandise as a gift. Using the U.S. mails to ship unordered merchandise also violates the Postal laws.

CHAPTER 13:
THE TELEMARKETING SALES RULE

OVERVIEW

In August 1994, the Telemarketing and Consumer Fraud and Abuse Prevention Act became law. The purposes of the Act are to combat the growth of telemarketing fraud by providing law enforcement agencies with powerful new tools, and to give consumers new protections and guidance on how to tell the difference between fraudulent and legitimate telemarketing.

Under the Act, the Federal Trade Commission (FTC) adopted the Telemarketing Sales Rule ("the Rule") on August 16, 1995, to achieve those goals. The Rule was effective on December 31, 1995. The key provisions of the Rule require specific disclosures, prohibit misrepresentations, set limits on the times telemarketers may call consumers, prohibit calls after a consumer asks not to be called, set payment restrictions for the sale of certain goods and services, and require that specific business records be kept for two years.

The Rule is not intended to affect any state or local telemarketing law. Therefore, an attorney general or other authorized state official may proceed with an action in state court to enforce any of that state's civil or criminal laws.

COVERED PRACTICES

The Telemarketing Sales Rule covers telemarketing—i.e., any plan, program, or campaign to sell goods or services through interstate telephone calls. With some important exceptions explained below, any persons or companies that take part in any plan, program, or campaign to sell goods or services through interstate telephone calls must comply with the Rule. This is true whether, as "telemarketers," they initiate or receive telephone calls to or from consumers, or whether, as "sellers," they provide, offer to provide, or arrange to provide goods or services to consumers in exchange for payment.

Some businesses and individuals are not covered by the Rule even though they may use interstate telephone calls to sell goods or services. The following four types of entities are not subject to the FTC's jurisdiction and therefore not covered by the Rule:

1. Banks, federal credit unions, and federal savings and loans;

2. Common carriers, such as long-distance telephone companies and airlines;

3. Non-profit organizations—i.e., entities that are not organized to carry on business for their own profit or that of their members; and

4. Companies engaged in the business of insurance, to the extent that this business is regulated by state law.

These four types of entities are not covered by the Rule only because they are specifically exempted from the FTC's jurisdiction; however, any other individual or company that contracts with one of these four types of entities to provide telemarketing services must comply with the Rule. For example, although banks are not covered by the Rule, a nonbank company that contracts with a bank to provide telemarketing services on behalf of the bank is covered. Similarly, a non-airline company that contracts with an airline to provide telemarketing services on behalf of the airline is covered by the Rule, and a company that is acting for profit may be covered by the Rule if it sells goods or services of more than nominal value on behalf of a nonprofit corporation.

In addition, under the provisions of the Telemarketing and Consumer Fraud and Abuse Prevention Act, a number of entities and individuals subject to the jurisdiction of the Securities and Exchange Commission (SEC) or the Commodity Futures Trading Commission are not covered by the Rule, even if they engage in a plan, program, or campaign to sell through interstate telephone calls.

Some types of calls also are not covered by the Rule, regardless of whether the business or individual making the call is covered, including:

1. Calls placed by consumers in response to a catalog—Generally, the Rule does not apply to calls placed by consumers in response to a catalog, so long as (a) the catalog contains a written description or illustration of the goods or services offered for sale; (b) the catalog includes the business address of the seller; (c) the catalog includes multiple pages of written material or illustrations; (d) the catalog has been issued not less frequently than once a year; and (e) the catalog seller does not solicit consumers by telephone but only receives calls initiated by consumers in response to the catalog, and during those calls from consumers takes orders only without further solicitation.;

2. 900-number calls—The Rule does not apply to 900-Number pay-per-call telephone calls, however, providers of pay-per-call services must comply with the FTC's 900-Number Rule;

3. Calls related to the sale of franchises or certain business opportunities—The Rule does not apply to calls relating to sales of franchises or business opportunities that are covered by the FTC's Franchise Rule, however, the Rule does apply to the telemarketing of business ventures not covered by the FTC's Franchise Rule.;

4. Unsolicited calls from consumers—Calls from consumers that are not the result of any solicitation by a seller or telemarketer are not covered by the Rule because they are not considered to be part of a telemarketing plan, program, or campaign to sell goods or services;

5. Calls that are part of a transaction that involves a face-to-face sales presentation—The Rule does not cover telephone transactions that are not completed until after a face-to-face sales presentation by the seller and the consumer is not required to pay or authorize payment until after such a presentation. The goal of the Rule is to protect consumers against deceptive or abusive practices that can arise in situations where the consumer has no direct contact—other than the telephone sales call itself—with an invisible and anonymous seller;

6. Business-to-business calls that do not involve retail sales of nondurable office or cleaning supplies—Most telephone calls between a telemarketer and a business are exempt from the Rule's coverage, however, business-to-business calls involving the retail sale of nondurable office or cleaning supplies are covered by the Rule;

7. Calls made in response to general media advertising—The Rule generally does not apply to consumer calls made in response to general media advertising, such as television commercials, infomercials, home shopping programs, magazine and newspaper advertisements, Yellow Pages or similar general directory listings, and other forms of mass media advertising and solicitations, however, the Rule does cover calls from consumers in response to general media advertisements relating to credit repair, recovery services, advance-fee loans, or investment opportunities; and

8. Calls made in response to direct mail advertising—Direct mail advertising includes any material—postcards, flyers, door hangers, brochures, "certificates," or letters—sent to a person urging that person to call a specified telephone number regarding an offer of some sort. However, there is no exemption for calls elicited by direct mail advertising that does not truthfully provide a consumer with the specific information required under the Rule nor is there any exemption for calls re-

sponding to any direct mail advertising that relates to credit repair, recovery services, advance-fee loans, investment opportunities, or prize promotions, regardless of whether the advertisement makes all the disclosures required by the Rule.

DISCLOSURE REQUIREMENT

The Rule requires a seller or telemarketer, whether making outbound calls to consumers or receiving inbound calls from consumers, to provide certain material information before that consumer pays for goods or services that are the subject of the sales offer. Material information is information that would likely affect a person's choice of goods or services, or their conduct regarding them—i.e., information necessary for a consumer to make an informed purchasing decision.

Sellers and telemarketers may provide the material information either orally or in writing. In the case of outbound calls, however, there are certain items of information that a telemarketer must promptly disclose to consumers orally in the sales presentation.

Failure to provide any of the required information in a "clear and conspicuous" manner, before the consumer pays for the goods or services offered, is a deceptive telemarketing act or practice that violates the Rule, and subjects a seller or telemarketer to a $10,000 fine for each violation.

The Rule specifies four broad categories of material information that sellers and telemarketers must provide to consumers:

1. Cost and Quantity—The Rule requires a seller or telemarketer to disclose the total costs to purchase, receive, or use the offered goods or services.

2. Material Restrictions, Limitations, or Conditions—The Rule requires sellers and telemarketers to disclose to a consumer all material restrictions, limitations, or conditions to purchase, receive, or use goods or services that the seller or telemarketer is offering to the consumer. As noted above, material information is information that a consumer needs to make an informed purchase decision.

3. No-Refund Policy—If the seller has a policy of honoring requests for refunds, cancellations of sales or orders, exchanges, or repurchases, the seller or telemarketer is required to disclose information about the policy only if the seller or telemarketer makes a statement about the policy during the sales presentation. If the seller has a policy of not giving refunds, not allowing cancellation of sales or orders, not providing exchanges for goods or services, or not repurchasing the offered goods

or services, the Rule requires the seller or telemarketer to inform consumers of this fact before they pay for the offered goods or services.

4. Prize Promotions—A "prize promotion" includes (1) any sweepstakes or other game of chance, and (2) any representation that a person has won, has been selected to receive, or may be eligible to receive a prize or purported prize. A "prize" is anything offered and given to a consumer by chance.

The Rule requires four prompt oral disclosures in outbound calls. An outbound call is a call initiated by a telemarketer to a consumer. The Rule requires that a telemarketer making an outbound call promptly disclose, in a clear and conspicuous manner, the following four items of information:

1. The identity of the seller. The seller is the entity that provides goods or services to the consumer in exchange for payment. The identity of the telemarketer, or person making the call, need not be disclosed if it is different from the identity of the seller.

2. That the purpose of the call is to sell goods or services.

3. The nature of the offered goods or services. This is a brief description of items offered for sale.

4. Required information about a prize promotion must be given before or in conjunction with the description of the prize offered.

MISREPRESENTATION

The Rule generally prohibits a seller or telemarketer from making any false or misleading statement to induce anyone to pay for goods or services. For example, telemarketers cannot falsely claim that they need to obtain a consumer's bank account number or credit card number only for identification purposes, when in fact they use those numbers to obtain payment for the goods or services offered. The Rule prohibits both express and implied misrepresentations. The seven categories of information that must not be misrepresented are set out below.

1. Cost and Quantity—The Rule prohibits a seller or telemarketer from misrepresenting the total costs to purchase, receive, or use the offered goods or services, or the quantity of goods or services offered at the stated price.

2. Material Restrictions, Limitations, or Conditions—The Rule prohibits sellers or telemarketers from misrepresenting any material restriction, limitation, or condition to purchase, receive, or use goods or services offered to the consumer.

3. Performance, Efficacy, or Central Characteristics—Sellers and telemarketers may not misrepresent any material aspect of the performance, efficacy, nature, or central characteristics of offered goods or services.

4. Refund, Repurchase, or Cancellation Policies—The Rule prohibits any seller or telemarketer from misrepresenting any material aspect—one that likely would have an effect on the consumer's purchasing decision—of the nature or terms of the seller's refund, cancellation, exchange, or repurchase policies.

5. Material Aspects of Prize Promotions -The Rule prohibits any seller or telemarketer from misrepresenting any material aspect of a prize promotion.

6. Material Aspects of Investment Opportunities—The Rule prohibits sellers and telemarketers from misrepresenting any material aspect of an investment opportunity.

7. Affiliations or Endorsements—The Rule prohibits any seller or telemarketer from misrepresenting their affiliation with, or endorsement by, any government or third-party organization.

ASSISTING AND FACILITATING VIOLATORS

It is a violation of the Rule for anyone to substantially assist a seller or telemarketer if that person knows or consciously avoids knowing that the seller or telemarketer is violating the Rule. A person violates the Rule if he or she knows of, or takes deliberate steps to ensure his or her own ignorance of, a seller's or telemarketer's Rule violations, yet helps the seller or telemarketer.

CREDIT CARD LAUNDERING

Credit card laundering is basically the misuse of what is known as a "merchant account" with a financial institution. A merchant account is a kind of bank account; it is what a seller or telemarketer needs in order to gain access to a credit card collection and payment system and to obtain cash for goods and services sold. Obtaining access to the credit card system through another's merchant account without the authorization of the financial institution is credit card laundering. Credit card laundering not only violates the Rule; it is a criminal offense under federal law, as well as the law of some states.

ABUSIVE PRACTICES

The Rule prohibits a seller or telemarketer from engaging in certain conduct that is classified as abusive, including threats, intimidation, or the use of profane or obscene language, and requesting or receiving payment for credit repair services or recovery services. Debt collection services are not covered by the Rule because they are not "conducted to induce the purchase of goods or services, however, debt collectors must comply with the FTC's Fair Debt Collection Practices Act.

CALLING RESTRICTIONS

The Rule imposes calling restrictions and prohibits telemarketers from:

1. Calling consumers repeatedly or continuously, with the intent to annoy, abuse, or harass any person at the called number;

2. Calling any consumer who previously has requested that he or she not be called again—the "do not call" provision as further discussed below; or

3. Calling any consumer's residence before 8:00 A.M. or after 9:00 PM. local time at the consumer's location.

The "Do Not Call" Provision

A telemarketer may not call a consumer who previously has requested to receive no more calls from, or on behalf of, a particular seller whose goods or services are being offered. Similarly, a seller that has been requested by a consumer not to call again may not cause a telemarketer to call that consumer.

Sellers and telemarketers are responsible for keeping "do not call lists" of those consumers who have requested not to receive calls placed by, or on behalf of, a particular seller. Calling a consumer who has requested not to be called is a Rule violation and a telemarketer or seller that engages in the practice of making such calls risks a $10,000 civil penalty per violation.

If a consumer is called who has requested not to be called by or on behalf of a particular seller, the seller and telemarketer may be liable for a Rule violation. If an enforcement investigation finds that neither the seller nor the telemarketer had written "do not call" procedures in place, both would be liable for the Rule violation. If the investigation reveals that the seller had written "do not call" procedures but the telemarketer ignored the procedures, the telemarketer would be liable for the Rule violation. The seller may also be liable if the investigation finds that the seller did not implement its written procedures. Ultimately a seller is responsible for keeping a current "do not call" list, whether it is through a telemarketing service it hires or through its own efforts.

If a seller or telemarketer has and implements written "do not call" procedures, it will not be liable for a Rule violation if a subsequent call is the result of error, but it may be subject to an enforcement investigation. The investigation would focus on the effectiveness of the procedures in place, how they are implemented, and if all personnel are trained in the "do not call" procedures. If there is a high incidence of "errors," it may be determined that the procedures are inadequate to comply with the Rule's "do not call " requirements and thus there is a Rule violation. On the other hand, if there is a low incidence of "errors," there may not be a Rule violation.

RECORDKEEPING REQUIREMENT

The Rule requires most sellers and telemarketers to keep certain records that relate to their telemarketing activities. The following records must be maintained for two years from the date that the record is produced:

1. Advertising and promotional materials;

2. Information about prize recipients;

3. Sales records;

4. Employee records; and

5. All verifiable authorizations for demand drafts.

Sellers and telemarketers may maintain the records in any manner, format, or place that they keep such records in the ordinary course of business, including in electronic storage, on microfiche, or on paper.

Absent a written agreement between the parties, or if the written agreement is unclear as to who must maintain the required records, the telemarketer must keep the employee records, while the seller is responsible for keeping the advertising and promotional materials, information on prize recipients, sales records, and verifiable authorizations.

ENFORCEMENT

The FTC, the states, and private persons may bring civil law enforcement actions in federal district courts to enforce the Rule. Actions by the states may be brought by either the attorney general of the state or by any other state officer authorized by the state to bring actions on behalf of its residents. Private persons may bring an action to enforce the Rule if they have suffered $50,000 or more in actual damages.

If a state official or private person brings a legal action under the Rule, they must provide written notice of their action to the FTC prior to filing a complaint, if feasible, or immediately upon instituting the action. The notice must include a copy of the complaint and any other pleadings to be filed with the court.

PENALTIES

Anyone who violates the Rule is subject to civil penalties of up to $10,000 per violation. In addition, violators may be subject to nation-wide injunctions that prohibit certain conduct, and may be required to pay redress to injured consumers.

CHAPTER 14:
BUYING AND SELLING ON THE INTERNET

ELECTRONIC PAYMENTS

Most internet consumers use credit cards to pay for their online purchases. However, the use of debit cards—e.g., automated teller machine (ATM) cards—for online purchases is becoming increasingly more common. A debit card authorizes the seller to debit the sale amount from the consumer's bank account electronically. Banks are also issuing debit cards that also "act" as credit cards—e.g., a "debit" MasterCard. The consumer chooses whether to select the debit or credit option at the point of purchase. Either way, the funds are deducted from the consumer's bank account. The attraction of the "debit/credit" card is that it is accepted more readily for purchases.

Other types of electronic payments include cards which allow the consumer to transfer cash value to the card. These are known as "stored value cards." For example, transportation systems often offer cards which are used to gain entry instead of purchasing individual tokens and, once depleted, funds can be added to the card for continued useage. Stores now offer gift certificates in the form of credit cards. The purchaser requests an amount which is then electronically stored on the card and the recipient uses the card as they would a credit card up to the cash value of the card. The card is then discarded.

Before purchasing a stored value card, the consumer should ask the issuer for written information about the product's features, including: the card's dollar limit; whether the card is reloadable or disposable; whether there is an expiration date; and any fees associated with the card.

A new type of internet-based payment system is called an "e-wallet." An e-wallet allows the consumer to establish an online account which is debited as the consumer makes on-line purchases. The consumer may use some form of stored value to establish the e-wallet account, or may set up an e-wallet account through a computer system connected to their credit or debit card account.

SECURE TRANSACTIONS

The consumer is advised to make sure that transactions made on-line are "secure"—i.e., the consumer's personal information is protected against fraud. Although it may be impossible to protect oneself completely from fraud and deception in both on-line and off-line purchases, there are some steps the consumer can take to make it less likely they will be a victim.

The consumer should make sure that they use a secure brower when making purchases on-line. A secure browser refers to software that encrypts or scrambles the purchase information sent over the Internet. One should be sure that the browser they use has the latest encryption capabilities available and should comply with industry security standards, such as Secure Sockets Layer (SSL). Most computers come with a browser installed. Some browsers are available for downloading over the internet at no cost to the consumer.

In addition, before providing personal financial information on a particular website, it is important to review the site's privacy policy to ascertain the security features offered by the site. Do not provide any private information if you are not satisfied that the site is secure.

SHIPPING COSTS AND REFUND POLICIES

When shopping on-line, it is important to find out the shipping and refund policies of the website where you are considering making purchases. Review all disclosures contained on the site. Once you order and receive the merchandise, you may find that the refund policies of the merchant are particularly restrictive or costly, at which time it may be simply too late to complain. It is best to do on-line business with reputable merchants with whom you are already familiar.

INVOICES AND RECEIPTS

Following your on-line purchase, the website usually generates a receipt or invoice which can be printed. The consumer should print out and retain this information and any other order confirmation sent by the merchant to the consumer's email address. This information should be checked against the consumer's monthly credit card and bank statements. Notify the credit card issuer or bank immediately if there are any discrepancies, errors, or unauthorized purchases.

In addition, the federal Mail/Telephone Order Merchandise Rule set forth in Chapter 12 covers online orders. This means that unless otherwise stated, merchandise must be delivered within 30 days, and if there are delays, the company must notify you.

THE ELECTRONIC FUND TRANSFER ACT (EFTA)

The Electronic Fund Transfer Act (EFTA) applies to electronic fund transfers—transactions involving automated teller machines (ATMs), debit cards and other point-of-sale debit transactions, and other electronic banking transactions that can result in the withdrawal of cash from the consumer's bank account.

Under the EFTA, procedures have been established for resolving errors on bank account statements, including: electronic fund transfers that the consumer did not make; electronic fund transfers that are incorrectly identified or show the wrong amount or date; computation or similar errors; the failure to properly reflect payments, credits, or electronic fund transfers; and electronic fund transfers for which the consumer requests an explanation or documentation, because of a possible error.

Under the EFTA, if there is a mistake or unauthorized withdrawal from your bank account through the use of a debit card, or other electronic fund transfers, you must notify your financial institution of the problem or error not later than 60 days after the statement containing the problem or error was sent. Although most financial institutions have a toll-free number to report the problem, you should follow up in writing.

For retail purchases, your financial institution has up to 10 business days to investigate after receiving your notice of the error. The financial institution must tell you the results of its investigation within three business days of completing its investigation. The error must be corrected within one business day after determining the error has occurred. If the institution needs more time, it may take up to 90 days to complete the investigation, but only if it returns the money in dispute to the customer's account within 10 business days after receiving notice of the error.

If someone uses a consumer's debit card, or makes other electronic fund transfers, without permission, the consumer can lose from $50 to $500 or more, depending on when they report the loss or theft. If the loss is reported within two business days after the problem is discovered, the consumer will not be responsible for more than $50 for unauthorized use. However, if the loss is not reported within two business days after the problem is discovered, but is reported within 60 days after the statement is mailed, the consumer could lose as much as $500 because of an unauthorized withdrawal. And, if the unauthorized transfer or withdrawal is not reported within 60 days after the statement is mailed, the consumer risks unlimited loss. That means the consumer could lose all the money in their account and the unused portion of their maximum line of credit established for overdrafts.

Some financial institutions may voluntarily cap a consumer's liability at $50 for certain types of transactions, regardless of when they report the loss or theft. However, because this protection is offered voluntarily, the policies could change at any time. Thus, the consumer is advised to ask their financial institution about its liability limits.

The EFTA may not cover stored-value cards or transactions involving them, so the consumer may not be covered for loss or misuse of such a card. Thus, a consumer should inquire as to whether the issuer offers any protection in the case of a lost, stolen, misused, or malfunctioning card.

E-MAIL SCAMS

According to the Federal Trade Commission (FTC), an increasing internet problem is the circulation of unsolicited commercial emails making fraudulent offers to consumers. The FTC has identified the twelve most likely email scams a consumer may receive:

Business Opportunities

Many business opportunity solicitations that claim to offer a way to make money in an internet-related business are actually illegal pyramid schemes masquerading as legitimate opportunities to earn money. These offers generally provide very little information and contain a telephone number to call for more details or ask the consumer to leave his or her number for a return phone call.

Bulk Email Solicitations

Bulk email solicitations offer lists of email addresses so the purchaser can send their own bulk email solicitations. However, most internet service providers prohibit bulk email solicitation and may discontinue the internet service of those who violate this prohibition. In addition, several states have laws regulating the sending of unsolicited commercial email, which may unintentionally be violated when bulk email solicitations are made.

Chain Letters

A chain letter generally requests the recipient to send a small amount of money to names provided on a list and then to add their own name in the place of one of those names and forward the letter on to a bulk mailing list. The idea is that the recipient will then receive money from those he or she solicits. Even though the chain letter may claim that the money-making scheme is legal, such plans are almost always illegal and are notorious for causing the participants to lose their money.

Work-at-Home Schemes

Work-at-home schemes often involve envelope stuffing. The recipient ends up investing money in equipment or supplies only to find out that there is no real employment offered but a scheme whereby the recipient is instructed on how to engage others in the same envelope-stuffing scam.

Health and Diet

All types of health cures and weight loss schemes are offered on the internet. Generally, they don't work and the ads are bolstered by false testimonials by allegedly "cured" consumers and so-called "famous" medical experts.

Get Rich Quick Schemes

Get-rich-quick schemes which describe a variety of easy-money making opportunities are also prevalent on the internet. They often request the consumer to send a small amount of money for details. These are scams which generally only make money for the solicitor.

Free Goods

Solicitations which offer valuable goods for free usually require the consumer to pay a fee to join a club and, in order to earn the free goods, to bring in a certain number of additional participants. Most of these messages are covering up pyramid schemes and almost all of the income, if any, goes to the solicitor and little or none to the consumers who pay to participate.

Investment Opportunities

Another scam to be aware of are investment schemes promising outrageously high rates of return with no risk. These schemes take many forms. Promoters of fraudulent investments often operate a particular scam for a short time, quickly spend the money they take in, then close down before they can be detected. Although the internet may contain many legitimate investment opportunities, it is impossible to completely root out all of the illegitimate and unscrupulous offers.

Some fraudulent investment promoters host websites that make their "investment company" look like a solid, top-rated Wall Street investment firm, featuring professional-looking sites that use classy graphics, audio and even video clips. The potential investor should proceed with extreme caution before submitting any personal information online to an investment promoter. The buyer's personal information may be used to develop a list of "leads" which are sold to other investment solicitors.

A list of organizations which provide the potential investor with information about investing on the internet is set forth at Appendix 8.

Cable Descrambler Kits

These offers involve the purchase of kits which purportedly allow the consumer to receive cable television transmission without paying a cable provider. Generally, the kits do not work and, even if it did, it is illegal to steal service from a cable television company.

Guaranteed Credit

There are many offers of loans, unsecured credit cards and other types of guaranteed credit on the internet. Generally, these offers are not legitimate.

Credit Repair

Credit repair scams offer to erase accurate negative information from your credit file so you can qualify for a credit card, auto loan, home mortgage, or a job. The companies that advertise credit repair services appeal to consumers with poor credit histories. Not only can't they provide you with a clean credit record, but they also may be encouraging you to violate federal law. If you follow their advice by lying on a loan or credit application, misrepresenting your Social Security number, or getting an Employer Identification Number from the Internal Revenue Service under false pretenses, you will be committing fraud.

Vacation Prize Promotions

Electronic certificates congratulating the consumer on "winning" a fabulous vacation for a very low price are among the many scams arriving via email. These unsolicited commercial emails are generally sent to thousands or millions of recipients at a time. However, the accommodations are usually limited and/or sub-standard and the scam is that the consumer will pay more for an upgrade or to schedule the vacation "award" at a more convenient time.

INTERNET ADVERTISING

Many of the general principles of advertising law apply to internet advertising, but new issues arise almost as fast as technology develops. The same consumer protection laws that apply to commercial activities in other media apply online. The FTC Act's prohibition on "unfair or deceptive acts or practices" encompasses internet advertising, marketing and sales.

A directory of companies which provide the consumer with information and assistance in resolving complaints about internet fraud is set forth at Appendix 9.

In addition, the Better Business Bureau has established a Code of Online Business Practices designed to guide ethical "business to customer" conduct in electronic commerce in order to boost customer trust and confidence in online commerce.

The text of the Better Business Bureau Code of Online Business Practices is set forth at Appendix 10.

Applicability of FTC Law to Internet Advertising

The FTC's role in protecting consumers from unfair or deceptive acts or practices encompasses advertising, marketing, and sales online, as well as the same activities in print, television, telephone and radio. Therefore, the plain language of many rules and guides applies to claims made on the Internet.

Required Disclosures

Disclosures that are required to prevent an ad from being misleading, to ensure that consumers receive material information about the terms of a transaction or to further public policy goals, must be clear and conspicuous. Information affecting the actual cost of an item offered on the internet should be disclosed on the same electronic page where the advertised price is located. Advertisers should not use pop-up windows or hyperlinks to other electronic pages to display such information. For example, where an offer advertises the availability of a rebate, where the rebate is dependent on the purchase of internet service, the cost of the Internet service should be disclosed on the same page as the advertised price of the computer.

When using a hyperlinked disclosure, advertisers should clearly label the hyperlink so it shows the importance, nature and relevance of the information to which it links. The hyperlink should be prominent, near the claim it is qualifying, easily noticeable, and lead directly to the qualifying information. In addition, information that is significant to the advertised offer should not be buried at the end of a long web page that requires consumers to scroll past unrelated information. Consumers should not have to wander through an electronic maze to discover important conditions or limitations of an offer.

The Mail or Telephone Order Merchandise Rule

As more fully set forth in Chapter 12, under the Mail or Telephone Order Merchandise Rule, all retailers, including "e-tailers"—i.e., on-line merchants—are required to ship an order within the time stated in their ads or on their website when the order is placed. A merchant must have a reasonable basis for stating that a product can be shipped within a certain time. If the advertisement doesn't clearly and prominently state the shipment period, the merchant must have a reasonable basis for believing that they can ship within 30 days. If the merchant cannot ship within the promised time—or within 30 days if no shipping date is promised—the merchant must notify the consumer of the delay, provide a revised shipment date and explain the consumer's right to cancel and get a full and prompt refund.

For definite delays of up to 30 days, the merchant may treat the consumer's silence as an agreement to the delay. But for longer or indefinite delays, and second and subsequent delays, the merchant must get the customer's written, electronic or verbal consent to the delay. If the customer does not agree, the merchant must promptly refund all the money the consumer paid whether or not a request was made.

The merchant has the right to cancel orders that he or she is unable to fill in a timely manner, but the merchant must promptly notify the consumer of the decision and make a prompt refund.

If a merchant is unexpectedly overwhelmed with orders, the merchant can change their shipment promises up to the point the consumer places the order, if the merchant reasonably believes it can ship by the new date. The updated information overrides previous promises and reduces the merchant's need to send delay notices. However, the consumer must be alerted to the new shipment date prior to taking the order.

The Mail or Telephone Order Rule is enforced by the Federal Trade Commission and applies to orders placed by phone, fax or the Internet. The Federal Trade Commission recently took action against seven "e-tailer" violators in "Project TooLate.Com." The FTC alleged that the e-tailers missed shipment deadlines for many holiday customers, failed to notify consumers of delays, and continued to promise timely deliveries even when huge backlogs of orders made it unlikely that the current orders would ship on time. In addition, some e-tailers cashed consumers' money orders or checks shortly after the orders were placed; in many cases, it was long before the shipments were made.

As a result of the FTC's initiative, the e-tailers agreed to pay more than $1.5 million in civil penalties or consumer redress and to abide by the FTC's Mail or Telephone Order Merchandise Rule in all future transactions.

The underlying concern is that consumers will lose confidence in the electronic marketplace if on-line merchants fail to timely ship merchandise ordered on the internet.

Endorsements and Testimonials

The FTC's Guides Concerning the Use of Endorsements and Testimonials in Advertising apply to endorsements, which are defined as "any advertising message . . . [that] consumers are likely to believe reflects the opinions, beliefs, findings, or experience of a party other than the sponsoring advertiser." The Guides refer to advertising without limiting the media in which it is disseminated, and therefore, encompass online ads.

The Telemarketing Sales Rule

Direct mail solicitations generally refer to promotional materials that consumers receive through traditional mail. With technological advances, however, these kinds of solicitations have moved online. Although the FTC's Telemarketing Sales Rule applies largely to telemarketing calls from business-to-consumer, it also applies to telephone calls the consumer places in response to a "direct mail" advertisement.

As with direct mail sent by traditional means, email can convey the false impression that the recipient has been selected for an offer not available to the general public. That impression may be exploited in a telemarketing call, particularly if the direct mail piece omits important information about the products or services offered. Therefore, if an email invites consumers to telephone the sender to purchase goods or services, the phone call is subject to the Telemarketing Sales Rule.

Nevertheless, not all online advertisements are considered "direct mail" solicitations. Telephone calls placed in response to general ads which do not appear to "specially select" the consumer would generally be exempt from the Telemarketing Sales Rule.

The Appliance Labeling Rule

On-line merchants that sell home appliances may be required to observe the FTC's Appliance Labeling Rule which requires manufacturers of certain appliances to affix yellow-and-black EnergyGuide labels to their appliances. It also requires appliance retailers to leave the labels in place. The labels give consumers information about the energy efficiency of competing models of appliances, and enable them to factor the cost of operating an appliance into their buying decisions. Consumers who purchase appliances through a website or catalog never come face-to-face with EnergyGuide labels. To ensure that these consumers have access to the energy efficiency information on the EnergyGuide labels before they buy, the FTC requires merchants to post the information on their sites.

The FTC's labeling and disclosure requirements apply to:

1. Refrigerators, freezers, dishwashers, clothes washers;

2. Water heaters, furnaces, boilers;

3. Central air conditioners, room air conditioners, heat pumps; and

4. Pool heaters.

Dealers who sell covered appliances online or through a catalog must disclose:

1. The capacity of the particular model.

2. For refrigerators, freezers, dishwashers, clothes washers and water heaters, the model's estimated annual energy consumption.

3. For air conditioners, heat pumps, furnaces, boilers and pool heaters, the energy efficiency rating.

4. The range of estimated annual energy consumption or energy efficiency ratings of comparable appliances.

Advertising On-Line and Children

The Children's Online Privacy Protection Act (COPPA) and the FTC's implementing Rule took effect April 21, 2000. The primary goal of the Act and the Rule is to place parents in control over what information is collected from their children online. The COPPA Rule applies to operators of commercial websites and online services directed to children under 13 that collect personal information from children, and operators of general audience sites with actual knowledge that they are collecting information from children under 13. Those operators must:

(1) post clear and comprehensive Privacy Policies on the website describing their information practices for children's personal information;

(2) provide notice to parents, and with limited exceptions, obtain verifiable parental consent before collecting personal information from children;

(3) give parents the choice to consent to the operator's collection and use of a child's information while prohibiting the operator from disclosing that information to third parties;

(4) provide parents access to their child's personal information to review and/or have it deleted;

(5) give parents the opportunity to prevent further collection or use of the information

(6) maintain the confidentiality, security, and integrity of information they collect from children.

In addition, the Rule prohibits operators from conditioning a child's participation in an online activity on the child's providing more information than is reasonably necessary to participate in that activity.

The Rule sets out a number of factors in determining whether a website is targeted to children, such as its subject matter, language, whether it uses animated characters, and whether advertising appearing on the site is directed to children. The Commission will also consider empirical evidence regarding the ages of the site's visitors. These standards are very similar to those previously established for TV, radio, and print advertising.

The FTC monitors the internet for compliance with the Rule and brings law enforcement actions where appropriate to deter violations. Parents and others can submit complaints to the FTC, and the FTC will also investigate referrals from consumer groups, industry, and approved safe harbor programs, as appropriate.

Website operators who violate the Rule could be liable for civil penalties of up to $11,000 *per violation*. The level of penalties assessed may turn on a number of factors including egregiousness of the violation, *e.g.*, the number of children involved, the amount and type of personal information collected, how the information was used, whether it was shared with third parties and the size of the company.

The text of the Children's Online Privacy Protection Act (COPPA) is set forth at Appendix 11.

INTERNET AUCTIONS

Internet auctions are some of the most popular events on the web. These auctions offer millions of buyers all kinds of merchandise from places all over the world. Sellers market everything from vintage toys found in their attic to complete computer systems and more. There is certain information one must know about how an internet auction works in order to successfully participate as a buyer or a seller.

First, one must make sure the particular auction website is reputable and determine how it operates its auctions. Different rules may apply from one site to another. Some auction sites offer tutorials to demonstrate the bidding process. Some auction sites also offer free insurance or other guarantees in case the seller fails to deliver the item or otherwise defrauds the buyer.

Internet auctions can be business-to-person or person-to-person. Operators of business-to-person auction sites have physical control of the merchandise being offered and accept payment for the goods. In person-to-person auctions, individual sellers or small businesses offer their items for auction directly to consumers. Generally, the seller has physical possession of the merchandise. After the auction closes, the seller is responsible for dealing directly with the highest bidder to arrange for payment and delivery.

Sellers usually auction one item at a time. In some cases, sellers offer multiple lots of the same item. These offers are known as "Dutch" or "English" auctions. At some sites, the seller may be required to sell all items at the price of the lowest successful bid. At other sites, the seller is entitled to the prices bid by each of the highest bidders.

A reserve price may be set by the seller which establishes the lowest price the seller is willing to accept. A closing time for the auction is set at which time the bidding ends and the highest bidder wins. If there are no bids that meet the reserve price, the auction closes without a successful bidder. Once the auction closes, if there is a successful bidder, the seller and buyer arrange for payment and delivery. This is generally accomplished via email.

Depending on the seller's requirements, buyers are generally given several methods of payment, such as by credit or debit card, personal check, money order or COD. Using a credit card gives the buyer the most protection. If you pay by credit or charge card online, your transaction will be protected by the Fair Credit Billing Act. Under this law, consumers have the right to dispute charges under certain circumstances and temporarily withhold payment while the creditor is investigating them. In the event of unauthorized use of your credit or charge card, you are generally held liable only for the first $50 in charges.

Some sellers agree to use an escrow service where, for a buyer-paid fee, the service accepts payment from the buyer in the form of a check, money order or credit card. The service releases the money to the seller only after the buyer receives and approves the merchandise.

Unfortunately, internet auction fraud has also emerged as a significant problem. This may occur when the seller fails to deliver the product or delivers something less valuable than what was advertised, when the seller doesn't deliver the item timely, and when the seller fails to disclose all of the relevant information about the product or the terms of its sale.

The buyer is advised to check the seller's feedback rating, which is often contained on the internet site. Previous buyers will provide comments about their dealings with the seller and transmit those comments to the site for future buyers. Prior to bidding, read the description of the item to make sure you know what you are attempting to purchase. Sellers often post photographs of the item along with a detailed description. Determine whether the product is new, used, refurbished, etc. The buyer can also generally email the seller with specific questions prior to bidding. The buyer should also determine who pays for shipping and delivery and whether the item can be returned if the buyer is not satisfied.

The buyer is cautioned not to bid on an item unless they plan to proceed with the purchase. If the buyer is the highest bidder, he or she is obligated to purchase the item or risk being barred from bidding on that auction site in the future. When bidding, the buyer should not divulge personal financial information, such as their bank account number or credit card information, or other personal information, such as their social security number. In addition, all information related to the sale should be kept in a safe place, including the item description and photos; the seller's identifying information, and any receipt that is available to show that the buyer was the successful bidder. Also print out and retain any emails sent or received among the buyer, seller and auction site.

The seller should make sure they provide bidders with an accurate description of the item they are selling, including all of the terms and conditions of the sale. Include photos of the item, if available. The seller should respond to any emails received by potential bidders concerning the item. Following a successful auction, the seller should contact the winning bidder as soon as possible to confirm the details of the sale, including method of payment and an estimated delivery date.

Federal law prohibits deceptive or misleading practices, including internet auctions. Thus, the seller is obligated to accurately advertise their product, and honestly disclose the terms and conditions of the sale. The seller is prohibited from advertising false testimonials about either the seller or his or her product. The seller is also prohibited from placing fake bids during the auction in order to drive up the price. The seller must establish the minimum bid he or she is willing to accept. The seller must also state whether the buyer is obligated to pay for shipping costs. In addition, a seller cannot offer illegal goods or services on the internet. Once the auction closes, the seller is obligated to ship the merchandise within a certain time period and, if unable to do so, must give the buyer the opportunity to cancel the sale. The seller should also keep all relevant information concerning the transaction, including copies of all emails sent or received among the buyer, seller and auction site.

THE INTERNATIONAL ON-LINE MARKETPLACE

The internet has expanded the consumer's on-line shopping to include the international marketplace. However, shopping electronically in other countries presents a number of questions regarding such issues as shipping costs, return policies and currency exchange rates. According to the Federal Trade Commission, when shopping in the international marketplace, the consumer should heed the following tips:

Identify the Company

It is important to know who you are dealing with and whether the company is legitimate. Inquire about where the company is located and how you can contact the company.

Identify the Product

Know what you are buying so that you are not surprised when the product arrives. Make sure that all of the product details are described in the offer and contact the company with any questions you may have prior to placing your order.

Determine the Costs

Prior to making the purchase, determine all of the terms, conditions and costs associated with the sale. Obtain an itemized list of all of the costs involved, the terms and expected date of delivery, methods of payment, type of currency used, and all other policies and conditions, such as the company's refund and return policy, and warranties, etc.

Secure On-Line Payments

Make sure that your on-line payment is made with a secure browser that encrypts your personal and financial information so it cannot be obtained for unlawful purposes.

Privacy Concerns

Make sure that the privacy of all of your personal information provided to the company in connection with the sale is maintained. Inquire about the company's privacy statement and whether the company shares its customer lists with other vendors. A privacy policy is a statement on a website describing what information about the consumer is collected by the site and how it is used. The company's policy statement is generally located on their website. Ideally, the policy is posted prominently and offers the consumer options about the use of your personal information. These options are called opt-in and opt-out. An opt-in choice means the website won't use the consumer's information unless he or she specifically agrees. An opt-out choice means the website can use the information unless the consumer specifically directs it not to use the information.

Problem Resolution

Make sure that the company has a commitment to customer satisfaction and problem resolution.

International Guidelines

The United States and 28 other countries, working together as members of the Organization for Economic Cooperation and Development, have signed on to new international guidelines to help address consumer concerns over doing internet shopping in an international marketplace. The guidelines:

1. Set out principles for voluntary "codes of conduct" for businesses involved in electronic commerce;

2. Offer guidance to governments in evaluating their consumer protection laws regarding electronic commerce; and,

3. Give consumers advice about what to expect and what to look for when shopping online.

The goal is to build consumer confidence in the global electronic marketplace by working to ensure that consumers are just as safe when shopping online as when shopping offline-no matter where they live or where the company they do business with is based. The guidelines call on participating governments to take steps to boost consumer confidence in the electronic marketplace. They encourage governments to evaluate their consumer protection laws to make sure they extend to online shopping, and to ensure that consumers have recourse if they are dissatisfied. They also recommend that governments work together to combat cross-border fraud and help establish a climate for electronic commerce that balances the needs and interests of businesses and consumers.

A list of governments that signed on to the international guidelines for internet shopping in the international marketplace is set forth at Appendix 12.

APPENDIX 1:
APPLICABLE SECTIONS OF THE RESTATEMENT SECOND OF THE LAW OF CONTRACTS

SECTION 205: DUTY OF GOOD FAITH AND FAIR DEALING

Every contract imposes upon each party a duty of good faith and fair dealing in its performance and its enforcement.

SECTION 206: INTERPRETATION AGAINST THE DRAFTSMAN

In choosing among the reasonable meanings of a promise or agreement or a term thereof, that meaning is generally preferred which operates against the party who supplies the words or from whom a writing otherwise proceeds.

SECTION 207: INTERPRETATION FAVORING THE PUBLIC

In choosing among the reasonable meanings of a promise or agreement or a term thereof, a meaning that serves the public interest is generally preferred.

SECTION 208: UNCONSCIONABLE CONTRACT OR TERM

If a contract or term thereof is unconscionable at the time the contract is made a court may refuse to enforce the contract, or may enforce the remainder of the contract without the unconscionable term, or may so limit the application of any unconscionable term as to avoid any unconscionable result.

APPENDIX 2:
DIRECTORY OF STATE CONSUMER PROTECTION AGENCIES

STATE	ADDRESS	TELEPHONE NUMBER
Alabama	Consumer Protection Division, Office of the Attorney General, 11 S. Union Street, Montgomery, AL 36130	205-261-7334
Alaska	Consumer Protection Section, Office of the Attorney General, 1031 W. 4th Avenue, Suite 110-B, Anchorage, AK 99501	907-279-0428
Arizona	Financial Fraud Division, Office of the Attorney General, 1275 W. Washington St., Phoenix, AZ 85007	602-542-3702
Arkansas	Consumer Protection Division, Office of the Attorney General, 200 Tower Building, 4th & Center Streets, Little Rock, AR 72201	501-682-2007
California	Public Inquiry Unit, Office of the Attorney General, 1515 K Street., Suite 511, Sacramento, CA 94244-2550	916-322-3360
California	Consumer Protection Division, Los Angeles City Attorney's Office, 200 N. Main Street, 1600 City Hall East, Los Angeles, CA 90012	213-485-4515
Colorado	Consumer Protection Unit, Office of the Attorney General, 1525 Sherman Street, 3rd Floor, Denver, CO 80203	303-866-5167

STATE	ADDRESS	TELEPHONE NUMBER
Connecticut	Department of Consumer Protection, 165 Capitol Avenue, Hartford, CT 06106	203-566-4999
Delaware	Division of Consumer Affairs, Department of Community Affairs, 820 N. French Street, 4th Floor, Wilmington, DE 19801	302-571-3250
District of Columbia	Department of Consumer & Regulatory Affairs, 614 H Street NW, Washington, DC 20001	202-737-7000
Florida	Division of Consumer Services, 218 Mayo Building, Tallahassee, FL 32399	904-488-2226
Georgia	Governor's Office of Consumer Affairs, 2 Martin Luther King Jr. Drive SE, Plaza Level, E Tower, Atlanta, GA 30334	404-656-7000
Hawaii	Office of Consumer Protection, 828 Fort St. Mall, Honolulu, HI 96812-3767	808-548-2560
Idaho	None Listed	
Illinois	Consumer Protection Division, Office of the Attorney General, 100 W. Randolph Street, 12th Floor, Chicago, IL 60601	312-917-3580
Indiana	Consumer Protection Division, Office of the Attorney General, 219 State House, Indianapolis, IN 46204	37-232-6330
Iowa	Consumer Protection Division, Office of the Attorney General, 1300 E. Walnut Street, 2nd Floor, Des Moines, IA 50319	515-281-5926
Kansas	Consumer Protection Division, Office of the Attorney General, Kansas Judicial Center, 2nd Floor, Topeka, KS 66612	913-296-3761
Kentucky	Consumer Protection Division, Office of the Attorney General, 209 St. Clair Street, Frankfort, KY 40601	502-564-2200

STATE	ADDRESS	TELEPHONE NUMBER
Louisiana	Consumer Protection Section, Office of the Attorney General, State Capitol Building, P.O. Box 94005, Baton Rouge, LA 70804	504-342-7013
Maine	Consumer and Antitrust Division, Office of the Attorney General, State House Station #6, Augusta, ME 04333	207-289-3716
Maryland	Consumer Protection Division, Office of the Attorney General, 7 N. Calvert Street, 3rd Floor, Baltimore, MD 21202	301-528-8662
Massachusetts	Consumer Protection Division, Office of the Attorney General, One Ashburton Place, Room 1411, Boston, MA 02108	617-727-7780
Michigan	Consumer Protection Division, Office of the Attorney General, 670 Law Building, Lansing, MI 48913	517-373-1140
Minnesota	Office of Consumer Services, Office of the Attorney General, 117 University Avenue, St. Paul, MN 55155	612-296-2331
Mississippi	Consumer Protection Division, Office of the Attorney General, P.O. Box 220, Jackson, MS 39205	601-359-3680
Missouri	Trade Offense Division, Office of the Attorney General, P.O. Box 899, Jefferson City, MO 65102	314-751-2616
Montana	Consumer Affairs Unit, Department of Commerce, 1424 9th Avenue, Helena, MT 59620	406-444-4312
Nebraska	Consumer Protection Division, Department of Justice, 2115 State Capitol, P.O. Box 98920, Lincoln, NE 68509	402-471-4723
Nevada	Department of Commerce, State Mail Room Complex, Las Vegas, NV 89158	702-486-4150

STATE	ADDRESS	TELEPHONE NUMBER
New Hampshire	Consumer Protection and Antitrust Division, Office of the Attorney General, State House Annex, Concord, NH 03301	603-271-3641
New Jersey	Division of Consumer Affairs, 1100 Raymond Boulevard, Room 504, Newark, NJ 07102	201-648-4010
New Mexico	Consumer and Economic Crime Division, Office of the Attorney General, P.O. Box Drawer 1508, Santa Fe, NM 87504	505-872-6910
New York	Consumer Protection Board, 99 Washington Avenue, Albany, NY 12210	518-474-8583
New York	Consumer Protection Board, 250 Broadway, 17th Floor, New York, NY 10007-2593	212-587-4908
North Carolina	Consumer Protection Section, Office of the Attorney General, P.O. Box 629, Raleigh, NC 27602	919-733-7741
North Dakota	Consumer Fraud Division, Office of the Attorney General, State Capitol Building, Bismarck, ND 58505	701-224-2210
Ohio	Consumer Frauds and Crimes Section, Office of the Attorney General, 30 E. Broad Street, 25th Floor, Columbus, OH 43266-0410	614-466-4986
Oklahoma	Consumer Affairs, Office of the Attorney General, 112 State Capitol Building, Oklahoma City, OK 73105	405-521-3921
Oregon	Financial Fraud Section, Office of the Attorney General, Justice Building, Salem, OR 97310	503-378-4320
Pennsylvania	Bureau of Consumer Protection, Office of the Attorney General, Strawberry Square, 14th Floor, Harrisburg, PA 17120	717-787-9707
Rhode Island	Consumer Protection Division, Office of the Attorney General, 72 Pine Street, Providence, RI 02903	401-277-2104

STATE	ADDRESS	TELEPHONE NUMBER
South Carolina	Department of Consumer Affairs, P.O. Box 5757, Columbia, SC 29250	803-734-9452
South Dakota	Division of Consumer Affairs, Office of the Attorney General, State Capitol Building, Pierre, SD 57501	605-773-4400
Tennessee	Division of Consumer Affairs, Department of Commerce & Insurance, 500 James Robertson Parkway, 5th Floor, Nashville, Tn 37219	615-741-4737
Texas	Consumer Protection Division, Office of the Attorney General, Box 12548, Capitol Station, Austin, TX 78711	512-463-2070
Utah	Division of Consumer Protection, Department of Business Regulation, 160 E. Third South, P.O. Box 45802, Salt Lake City, UT 84145	801-530-6601
Vermont	Public Protection Division, Office of the Attorney General, 109 State Street, Montpelier, VT 05602	802-828-3171
Virginia	Division of Consumer Counsel, Office of the Attorney General, Supreme Court Building, 101 N. 8th Street, Richmond, VA 23219	804-786-2116
Washington	Consumer and Business Fair Practices Division, 710 2nd Avenue, Suite 1300, Seattle, WA 98104	206-464-7744
West Virginia	Consumer Protection Division, Office of the Attorney General, 812 Quarrier Street, 6th Floor, Charleston, WV 25301	304-348-8986
Wisconsin	Office of Consumer Protection, Department of Justice, P.O. Box 7856, Madison, WI 53707	608-266-1852
Wyoming	Office of the Attorney General, 123 State Capitol Building, Cheyenne, WY 82002	307-777-6286*

Source: Consumers Resource Handbook U.S. Office of Consumer Affairs 1990.

APPENDIX 3:
STATE STATUTES GOVERNING UNFAIR AND DECEPTIVE ACTS AND PRACTICES

STATE	STATUTE	COMMENTS
Alabama	Ala Code § 8-19-1	Prohibits unconscionable or deceptive practices including 21 enumerated practices. Violations must be knowing.
Alaska	Alaska Stat. § 45.50.471	Prohibits unfair methods of competition and unfair or deceptive acts and practices including 28 enumerated practices.
Arizona	Ariz. Rev. Stat. Ann. § 44-1521	Prohibits deceptive practices and omissions of material fact with intent.
Arkansas	Ark. Stat. Ann § 4-88-101	Prohibits deceptive practices including 7 enumerated practices, and omissions of material fact with intent to cause reliance.
California	Cal. Civ. Code § 1750	Prohibits unfair methods of competition and unfair or deceptive practices including 22 enumerated practices. Violation must be intentional.
Colorado	Colo. Rev. Stat. § 6-1-101	Prohibits deceptive practices including 30 enumerated practices.
Connecticut	Conn. Gen. Stat. § 42-110a	Prohibits unfair methods of competition and unfair or deceptive acts or practices.

STATE	STATUTE	COMMENTS
Delaware	Del. Code Ann. Tit. 6 § 2511 and § 2531	Prohibits deceptive practices or omissions of material fact with intent to cause reliance including 11 enumerated practices, and other conduct creating a likelihood of misunderstanding.
District of Columbia	D.C. Code Ann. § 28-3901	Prohibits deceptive, unfair or unlawful trade practices including 26 enumerated practices, and unconscionable terms.
Florida	Fla. Stat. Ann. § 501.201	Prohibits unfair methods of competition and unfair or deceptive acts or practices.
Georgia	Ga. Code Ann. § 10-1-370 and § 10-1-390	Prohibits deceptive practices and conduct likely to create misunderstanding including 11 enumerated practices, and unfair or deceptive acts or practices in consumer transactions or office supply transactions.
Hawaii	Haw. Rev. Stat. § 480 and § 481A	Prohibits unfair methods of competition and unfair or deceptive trade practices including 11 enumerated deceptive practices, and conduct creating misunderstanding.
Idaho	Idaho Code § 48-601	Prohibits unfair methods of competition and unfair or deceptive acts or practices including 16 enumerated practices, and prohibits misleading consumer practice and any unconscionable practice. Violators must know or should know about violation.
Illinois	Ill. Rev. Stat. Ch. 121 1/2 § 261 and § 311	Prohibits unfair methods of competition and unfair or deceptive acts or practices including concealment or omission of any material fact with the intent to cause reliance including 15 enumerated prohibitions, and 11 enumerated deceptive trade practices and other conduct likely to cause confusion.

STATE	STATUTE	COMMENTS
Indiana	Ind. Code Ann. § 24-5-0.5-1	Prohibits numerous enumerated deceptive acts concerning consumer transactions including transactions involving contracts with unconscionable clauses.
Iowa	Iowa Code Ann. § 714.16	Prohibits unfair or deceptive acts including 4 enumerated practices, or concealment, suppression or omissions of material fact with intent to cause reliance.
Kansas	Kan. Stat. Ann. § 50-623	Prohibits any deceptive acts or practices or omissions as to a material fact including 10 enumerated prohibitions, and unconscionable practices including 7 enumerated prohibitions concerning consumer transactions, and seller must know or have reason to know of violation of deceptive practice.
Kentucky	Ky. Rev. Stat. § 367.110	Prohibits unfair or deceptive acts or practices where unfair is construed to mean unconscionable.
Louisiana	La. Rev. Stat. Ann. § 51:1401	Prohibits unfair methods of competition and unfair or deceptive acts or practices.
Maine	Me. Rev. Stat. Ann. Tit. 5 § 206 and Tit. 10 § 1211	Prohibits unfair methods of competition and unfair or deceptive acts or practices including 11 enumerated deceptive practices and prohibition of conduct likely to create confusion or misunderstanding.
Maryland	Md. Com. Law Code Ann. § 13-101	Prohibits numerous enumerated unfair or deceptive trade practices.
Massachusetts	Mass. Gen. Laws Ann. Ch. 93A	Prohibits unfair methods of competition and unfair or deceptive acts or practices.
Michigan	Mich. Comp. Laws Ann. § 445.901	Prohibits unfair, unconscionable or deceptive practices including 29 enumerated practices.

STATE	STATUTE	COMMENTS
Minnesota	Minn. Stat. Ann. §§ 8.31, § 325D.44, § 325F.67, , and § 325F.69	Prohibits unfair, discriminatory and other unlawful practices including 13 enumerated deceptive practices, conduct which simultaneously creates a likelihood of confusion or misunderstanding, untrue deceptive or misleading advertising, and fraud, misrepresentation and misleading statements.
Mississippi	Miss. Code Ann. § 75-24-1	Prohibits unfair methods of competition and unfair or deceptive acts or practices including 11 enumerated practices.
Missouri	Mo. Rev. Stat. § 407.010	Prohibits deceptive acts or concealment or omissions of material fact with intent to cause reliance.
Montana	Mont. Code Ann. § 30-14-101	Prohibits unfair methods of competition and unfair or deceptive acts or practices.
Nebraska	Neb. Rev. Stat. § 59-1601 and § 87-302	Prohibits unfair methods of competition and unfair or deceptive acts or practices including 14 enumerated practices and all unconscionable acts by suppliers in consumer transactions.
Nevada	Nev. Rev. Stat. § 41.600 and § 598.360	Prohibits 17 enumerated deceptive trade practices.
New Hampshire	N.H. Rev. Stat. Ann. § 358-A:1	Prohibits unfair methods of competition and unfair or deceptive acts or practices including 12 enumerated prohibitions.
New Jersey	N.J. Stat. Ann. § 56:8-1	Prohibits unconscionable commercial practice, deception, fraud or knowing concealment, and suppression or omission of material fact with intent to cause reliance including numerous enumerated prohibitions.
New Mexico	N.M. Stat. Ann. § 57-12-1	Prohibits unfair or deceptive trade practices including 17 enumerated prohibitions and 2 enumerated unconscionable trade practices.

STATE	STATUTE	COMMENTS
New York	N.Y. Exec. Law § 63(12) and N.Y. Gen. Bus. Law § 349 and § 350	Prohibits repeated fraudulent or illegal acts including deception, suppression or unconscionable contractual provisions, and deceptive acts or practices including false advertising.
North Carolina	N.C. Gen. Stat. § 75-1.1	Prohibits unfair methods of competition and unfair or deceptive acts or practices.
North Dakota	N.D. Gen. Stat. § 51-15-01	Prohibits deceptive practices with intent to cause reliance.
Ohio	Ohio Rev. Code Ann. § 1345.01 and § 4165	Prohibits unfair and deceptive acts or practices including 11 enumerated practices, and any unconscionable acts or practices including 7 enumerated examples.
Oklahoma	Okla. Stat. Ann. Tit. 15 § 751 and Tit. 78 § 51	Prohibits 17 enumerated unlawful practices and 11 enumerated deceptive trade practices.
Oregon	Or. Rev. Stat. § 646.605	Prohibits 2 enumerated unconscionable tactics and 20 enumerated unfair or deceptive acts or practices including any violation of attorney general UDAP rules.
Pennsylvania	Pa. Stat. Ann. Tit. 73 § 201-1	Prohibits 15 enumerated unfair methods of competition and unfair or deceptive acts or practices and any other conduct likely to create confusion.
Rhode Island	R.I. Gen. Law § 6-13.1-1	Prohibits 17 enumerated unfair methods of competition and unfair or deceptive practices.
South Carolina	S.C. Code Ann. § 39-5-10	Prohibits unfair methods of competition and unfair or deceptive acts or practices.
South Dakota	S.D. Codified Laws Ann. § 37-24-1	Prohibits deceptive acts or practices including 14 enumerated prohibitions.
Tennessee	Tenn. Code Ann. § 47-18-101	Prohibits unfair or deceptive acts or practices including 20 enumerated prohibitions and any other deceptive consumer act.

STATE	STATUTE	COMMENTS
Texas	Tex. Bus. , Com. Code Ann. § 17.41	Prohibits deceptive acts or practices including 23 enumerated prohibitions.
Utah	Utah Code Ann. §§ 13-2-1, 13-5-1, and 13-11-1	Prohibits unfair methods of competition including many enumerated unlawful practices, and prohibits deceptive acts or practices by a supplier in consumer transactions including 14 enumerated prohibitions and unconscionable practices by suppliers in consumer transactions.
Vermont	Vt. Stat. Ann. Tit. 9 § 2451	Prohibits unfair methods of competition and unfair or deceptive acts or practices.
Virginia	Va. Code § 59.1-196	Prohibits 24 enumerated fraudulent acts.
Washington	Wash. Rev. Code Ann. § 19.86.010	Prohibits unfair methods of competition and unfair or deceptive acts. Violations must be injurious to the public interest.
West Virginia	W. Va. Code § 46A-6-101	Prohibits unfair methods of competition and unfair or deceptive acts or practices.
Wisconsin	Wis. Stat. Ann. § 100.18 and § 100.20	Prohibits untrue, deceptive or misleading representations including 14 itemized deceptive representations, and unfair methods of competition and unfair trade practices.
Wyoming	Wyo. Stat. § 40-12-101	Prohibits enumerated practices plus other unfair or deceptive acts or practices. Violations must be knowing.

APPENDIX 4:
APPLICABLE SECTIONS OF THE RESTATEMENT THIRD OF THE LAW OF UNFAIR COMPETITION

SECTION 2: DECEPTIVE MARKETING: GENERAL PRINCIPLE

One who, in connection with the marketing of goods or services, makes a representation relating to the actor's own goods, services, or commercial activities that is likely to deceive or mislead prospective purchasers to the likely commercial detriment of another under the rule stated in Section 3 is subject to liability to the other for the relief appropriate under the rules stated in Sections 35-37.

SECTION 3: COMMERCIAL DETRIMENT OF ANOTHER

A representation is to the likely commercial detriment of another if:

(a) the representation is material, in that it is likely to affect the conduct of prospective purchasers; and

(b) there is a reasonable basis for believing that the representation has caused or is likely to cause a diversion of trade from the other or harm to the other's reputation or good will.

SECTION 4: MISREPRESENTATIONS RELATING TO SOURCE: PASSING OFF

One is subject to liability to another under the rule stated in Section 2 if, in connection with the marketing of goods or services, the actor makes a representation likely to deceive or mislead prospective purchasers by causing the mistaken belief that the actor's business is the business of the other, or that the actor is the agent, affiliate, or associate of the other, or that the goods or services that the actor markets are produced, sponsored, or approved by the other.

SECTION 5: MISREPRESENTATIONS RELATING TO SOURCE: REVERSE PASSING OFF

One is subject to liability to another under the rule stated in Section 2 if, in marketing goods or services manufactured, produced, or supplied by the other, the actor makes a representation likely to deceive or mislead prospective purchasers by causing the mistaken belief that the actor or a third person is the manufacturer, producer, or supplier of the goods or services if the representation is to the likely commercial detriment of the other under the rule stated in Section 3.

SECTION 6: MISREPRESENTATIONS IN MARKETING THE GOODS OR SERVICES OF ANOTHER

One is subject to liability to another under the rule stated in Section 2 if, in marketing goods or services of which the other is truthfully identified as the manufacturer, producer, or supplier, the actor makes a representation relating to those goods or services that is likely to deceive or mislead prospective purchasers to the likely commercial detriment of the other under the rule stated in Section 3.

SECTION 7: CONTRIBUTORY LIABILITY OF PRINTERS, PUBLISHERS, AND OTHER SUPPLIERS

(1) One who, by supplying materials or rendering services to a third person, directly and substantially assists the third person in making a representation that subjects the third person to liability to another for deceptive marketing under the rules stated in Sections 2-6 is subject to liability to that other for contributory deceptive marketing.

(2) If an actor subject to contributory liability under the rule stated in Subsection (1) acted without knowledge that the actor was assisting the third person in making a representation likely to deceive or mislead, the actor is subject only to appropriate injunctive relief.

SECTION 8: CONTRIBUTORY LIABILITY OF MANUFACTURERS AND DISTRIBUTORS

One who markets goods or services to a third person who further markets the goods or services in a manner that subjects the third person to liability to another for deceptive marketing under the rules stated in Sections 2-6 is subject to liability to that other for contributory deceptive marketing if:

(a) the actor intentionally induces the third person to engage in such conduct; or

(b) the actor fails to take reasonable precautions against the occurrence of the third person's conduct in circumstances in which that conduct can be reasonably anticipated.

SECTION 36: DAMAGES: TRADEMARK INFRINGEMENT AND DECEPTIVE MARKETING

(1) One who is liable to another for deceptive marketing under the rules stated in Sections 2-8 or for infringement of the other's trademark, trade name, collective mark, or certification mark under the rule stated in Section 20 is liable for the pecuniary loss to the other caused by the deceptive marketing or infringement, unless an award of damages for such pecuniary loss is prohibited by statute or is otherwise inappropriate under the rule stated in Subsection (3).

(2) The pecuniary loss for which damages may be recovered under this Section includes:

(a) loss resulting to the plaintiff from sales or other revenues lost because of the actor's conduct;

(b) loss resulting from sales made by the plaintiff at prices that have been reasonably reduced because of the actor's conduct;

(c) harm to the market reputation of the plaintiff's goods, services, business, or trademark; and

(d) reasonable expenditures made by the plaintiff in order to prevent, correct, or mitigate the confusion or deception of prospective purchasers resulting from the actor's conduct.

(3) Whether an award of damages for pecuniary loss is appropriate depends upon a comparative appraisal of all the factors of the case, including the following primary factors:

(a) the degree of certainty with which the plaintiff has established the fact and extent of the pecuniary loss caused by the actor's conduct;

(b) the relative adequacy to the plaintiff of other remedies, including an accounting of the actor's profits;

(c) the intent of the actor and the extent to which the actor knew or should have known that the conduct was unlawful;

(d) the role of the actor in bringing about the infringement or deceptive marketing;

(e) any unreasonable delay by the plaintiff in bringing suit or otherwise asserting its rights; and

(f) any related misconduct on the part of the plaintiff.

SECTION 37: ACCOUNTING OF DEFENDANT'S PROFITS: TRADEMARK INFRINGEMENT AND DECEPTIVE MARKETING

(1) One who is liable to another for deceptive marketing under the rules stated in Sections 2-8 or for infringement of the other's trademark, trade name, collective mark, or certification mark under the rule stated in Section 20 is liable for the net profits earned on profitable transactions resulting from the unlawful conduct, but only if:

(a) the actor engaged in the conduct with the intention of causing confusion or deception; and

(b) the award of profits is not prohibited by statute and is otherwise appropriate under the rule stated in Subsection (2).

(2) Whether an award of profits is appropriate depends upon a comparative appraisal of all the factors of the case, including the following primary factors:

(a) the degree of certainty that the actor benefitted from the unlawful conduct;

(b) the relative adequacy to the plaintiff of other remedies, including an award of damages;

(c) the interests of the public in depriving the actor of unjust gains and discouraging unlawful conduct;

(d) the role of the actor in bringing about the infringement or deceptive marketing;

(e) any unreasonable delay by the plaintiff in bringing suit or otherwise asserting its rights; and

(f) any related misconduct on the part of the plaintiff.

APPENDIX 5:
THE MAIL OR TELEPHONE ORDER
MERCHANDISE RULE

SEC. 435.1 THE RULE.

In connection with mail or telephone-order sales in or affecting commerce, as "commerce" is defined in the Federal Trade Commission Act, it constitutes an unfair method of competition, and an unfair or deceptive act or practice for a seller:

(a)(1) To solicit any order for the sale of merchandise to be ordered by the buyer through the mails or by telephone unless, at the time of the solicitation, the seller has a reasonable basis to expect that it will be able to ship any ordered merchandise to the buyer:

(i) Within that time clearly and conspicuously stated in any such solicitation, or

(ii) if no time is clearly and conspicuously stated, within thirty (30) days after receipt of a properly completed order from the buyer. Provided, however, Where, at the time the merchandise is ordered buyer applies to the seller for credit to pay for the merchandise in whole or in part, the seller shall have 50 days, rather than 30 days, to perform the actions required in § 435.1 (a)(1)(ii) of this part.

(2) To provide any buyer with any revised shipping date, as provided in paragraph (b) of this section, unless, at the time any such revised shipping date is provided, the seller has a reasonable basis for making such representation regarding a definite revised shipping date.

(3) To inform any buyer that it is unable to make any representation regarding the length of any delay unless

(i) the seller has a reasonable basis for so informing the buyer and

(ii) the seller informs the buyer of the reason or reasons for the delay.

---

(4) In any action brought by the Federal Trade Commission alleging a violation of this part, the failure of a respondent-seller to have records or other documentary proof establishing its use of systems and procedures which assure the shipment of merchandise in the ordinary course of business within any applicable time set forth in this part will create a rebuttable presumption that the seller lacked a reasonable basis for any expectation of shipment within said applicable time.

(b)(1) Where a seller is unable to ship merchandise within the applicable time set forth in paragraph (a)(1) of this section, to fail to offer to the buyer, clearly and conspicuously and without prior demand, an option either to consent to a delay in shipping or to cancel the buyer's order and receive a prompt refund. Said offer shall be made within a reasonable time after the seller first becomes aware of its inability to ship within the applicable time set forth in paragraph (a)(1) of this section, but in no event later than said applicable time.

(i) Any offer to the buyer of such an option shall fully inform the buyer regarding the buyer's right to cancel the order and to obtain a prompt refund and shall provide a definite revised shipping date, but where the seller lacks a reasonable basis for providing a definite revised shipping date the notice shall inform the buyer that the seller is unable to make any representation regarding the length of the delay.

(ii) Where the seller has provided a definite revised shipping date which is thirty (30) days or less later than the applicable time set forth in paragraph (a)(1) of this section, the offer of said option shall expressly inform the buyer that, unless the seller receives, prior to shipment and prior to the expiration of the definite revised shipping date, a response from the buyer rejecting the delay and cancelling the order, the buyer will be deemed to have consented to a delayed shipment on or before the definite revised shipping date.

(iii) Where the seller has provided a definite revised shipping date which is more than thirty (30) days later than the applicable time set forth in paragraph (a)(1) of this section or where the seller is unable to provide a definite revised shipping date and therefore informs the buyer that it is unable to make any representation regarding the length of the delay, the offer of said option shall also expressly inform the buyer that the buyer's order will automatically be deemed to have been cancelled unless:

(A) the seller has shipped the merchandise within thirty (30) days of the applicable time set forth in paragraph (a)(1) of this section, and has received no cancellation prior to shipment, or

(B) the seller has received from the buyer within thirty (30) days of said applicable time, a response specifically consenting to said shipping delay. Where the seller informs the buyer that it is unable to make any representation regarding the length of the delay, the buyer shall be expressly informed that, should the buyer consent to an indefinite delay, the buyer will have a continuing right to cancel the buyer's order at any time after the applicable time set forth in paragraph (a)(1) of this section by so notifying the seller prior to actual shipment.

(iv) Nothing in this paragraph shall prohibit a seller who furnishes a definite revised shipping date pursuant to paragraph (b)(1)(i) of this section, from requesting, simultaneously with or at any time subsequent to the offer of an option pursuant to paragraph (b)(1) of this section, the buyer's express consent to a further unanticipated delay beyond the definite revised shipping date in the form of a response from the buyer specifically consenting to said further delay. Provided, however, That where the seller solicits consent to an unanticipated indefinite delay the solicitation shall expressly inform the buyer that, should the buyer so consent to an indefinite delay, the buyer shall have a continuing right to cancel the buyer's order at any time after the definite revised shipping date by so notifying the seller prior to actual shipment.

(2) Where a seller is unable to ship merchandise on or before the definite revised shipping date provided under paragraph (b)(1)(i) of this section and consented to by the buyer pursuant to paragraph (b)(1)(ii) or (iii) of this section, to fail to offer to the buyer, clearly and conspicuously and without prior demand, a renewed option either to consent to a further delay or to cancel the order and to receive a prompt refund. Said offer shall be made within a reasonable time after the seller first becomes aware of its inability to ship before the said definite revised date, but in no event later than the expiration of the definite revised shipping date: Provided, however, That where the seller previously has obtained the buyer's express consent to an unanticipated delay until a specific date beyond the definite revised shipping date, pursuant to paragraph (b)(1)(iv) of this section or to a further delay until a specific date beyond the definite revised shipping date pursuant to paragraph (b)(2) of this section, that date to which the buyer has expressly consented shall supersede the definite revised shipping date for purposes of paragraph (b)(2) of this section.

(i) Any offer to the buyer of said renewed option shall provide the buyer with a new definite revised shipping date, but where the seller lacks a reasonable basis for providing a new definite revised shipping date, the notice shall inform the buyer that the seller is unable to make any representation regarding the length of the further delay.

(ii) The offer of a renewed option shall expressly inform the buyer that, unless the seller receives, prior to the expiration of the old definite revised shipping date or any date superseding the old definite revised shipping date, notification from the buyer specifically consenting to the further delay, the buyer will be deemed to have rejected any further delay, and to have cancelled the order if the seller is in fact unable to ship prior to the expiration of the old definite revised shipping date or any date superseding the old definite revised shipping date. Provided, however, That where the seller offers the buyer the option to consent to an indefinite delay the offer shall expressly inform the buyer that, should the buyer so consent to an indefinite delay, the buyer shall have a continuing right to cancel the buyer's order at any time after the old definite revised shipping date or any date superseding the old definite revised shipping date.

(iii) Paragraph (b)(2) of this section shall not apply to any situation where a seller, pursuant to the provisions of paragraph (b)(1)(iv) of this section, has previously obtained consent from the buyer to an indefinite extension beyond the first revised shipping date.

(3) Wherever a buyer has the right to exercise any option under this part or to cancel an order by so notifying the seller prior to shipment, to fail to furnish the buyer with adequate means, at the seller's expense, to exercise such option or to notify the seller regarding cancellation. Nothing in paragraph (b) of this section shall prevent a seller, where it is unable to make shipment within the time set forth in paragraph (a)(1) of this section or within a delay period consented to by the buyer, from deciding to consider the order cancelled and providing the buyer with notice of said decision within a reasonable time after it becomes aware of said inability to ship, together with a prompt refund.

(c) To fail to deem an order cancelled and to make a prompt refund to the buyer whenever:

(1) The seller receives, prior to the time of shipment, notification from the buyer cancelling the order pursuant to any option, renewed option or continuing option under this part;

(2) The seller has, pursuant to paragraph (b)(1)(iii) of this section, provided the buyer with a definite revised shipping date which is more than thirty (30) days later than the applicable time set forth in paragraph (a)(1) of this section or has notified the buyer that it is unable to make any representation regarding the length of the delay and the seller

(i) has not shipped the merchandise within thirty (30) days of the applicable time set forth in paragraph (a)(1) of this section, and

(ii) has not received the buyer's express consent to said shipping delay within said thirty (30) days;

(3) The seller is unable to ship within the applicable time set forth in paragraph (b)(2) of this section, and has not received, within the said applicable time, the buyer's consent to any further delay;

(4) The seller has notified the buyer of its inability to make shipment and has indicated its decision not to ship the merchandise;

(5) The seller fails to offer the option prescribed in paragraph (b)(1) of this section and has not shipped the merchandise within the applicable time set forth in paragraph (a)(1) of this section.

(d) In any action brought by the Federal Trade Commission, alleging a violation of this part, the failure of a respondent-seller to have records or other documentary proof establishing its use of systems and procedures which assure compliance, in the ordinary course of business, with any requirement of paragraph (b) or (c) of this section will create a rebuttable presumption that the seller failed to comply with said requirement.

SEC. 435.2 DEFINITIONS.

For purposes of this part:

(a) "Mail or telephone order sales" shall mean sales in which the buyer has ordered merchandise from the seller by mail or telephone, regardless of the method of payment or the method used to solicit the order.

(b) "Telephone" refers to any direct or indirect use of the telephone to order merchandise, regardless of whether the telephone is activated by, or the language used is that of human beings, machines, or both.

(c) "Shipment" shall mean the act by which the merchandise is physically placed in the possession of the carrier.

(d) "Receipt of a properly completed order" shall mean, where the buyer tenders full or partial payment in the proper amount in the form of cash, check, money order, or authorization from the buyer to charge an existing charge account, the time at which the seller receives both said payment and an order from the buyer containing all of the information needed by the seller to process and ship the order. Provided, however, That where the seller receives notice that the check or money order tendered by the buyer has been dishonored or that the buyer does not qualify for a credit sale, "receipt of a properly completed order" shall mean the time at which:

(i) the seller receives notice that a check or money order for the proper amount tendered by the buyer has been honored,

(ii) the buyer tenders cash in the proper amount or

(iii) the seller receives notice that the buyer qualifies for a credit sale.

(e) "Refund" shall mean:

(1) Where the buyer tendered full payment for the unshipped merchandise in the form of cash, check or money order, a return of the amount tendered in the form of cash, check or money order;

(2) Where there is a credit sale:

(i) And the seller is a creditor, a copy of a credit memorandum or the like or an account statement reflecting the removal or absence of any remaining charge incurred as a result of the sale from the buyer's account;

(ii) And a third party is the creditor, a copy of an appropriate credit memorandum or the like to the third party creditor which will remove the charge from the buyer's account or a statement from the seller acknowledging the cancellation of the order and representing that it has not taken any action regarding the order which will result in a charge to the buyer's account with the third party;

(iii) And the buyer tendered partial payment for the unshipped merchandise in the form of cash, check or money order, a return of the amount tendered in the form of cash, check or money order.

(f) "Prompt refund" shall mean:

(1) Where a refund is made pursuant to paragraph (e)(1) or (2)(iii) of this section, a refund sent to the buyer by first class mail within seven (7) working days of the date on which the buyer's right to refund vests under the provisions of this part;

(2) Where a refund is made pursuant to paragraph (e)(2)(i) or (ii) of this section, a refund sent to the buyer by first class mail within one (1) billing cycle from the date on which the buyer's right to refund vests under the provisions of this part.

(g) The "time of solicitation" of an order shall mean that time when the seller has:

(1) Mailed or otherwise disseminated the solicitation to a prospective purchaser,

(2) Made arrangements for an advertisement containing the solicitation to appear in a newspaper, magazine or the like or on radio or television which cannot be changed or cancelled without incurring substantial expense, or

(3) Made arrangements for the printing of a catalog, brochure or the like which cannot be changed without incurring substantial expense, in which the solicitation in question forms an insubstantial part.

SEC. 435.3 LIMITED APPLICABILITY.

(a) This part shall not apply to:

(1) Subscriptions, such as magazine sales, ordered for serial delivery, after the initial shipment is made in compliance with this part.

(2) Orders of seeds and growing plants.

(3) Orders made on a collect-on-delivery (C.O.D.) basis.

(4) Transactions governed by the Federal Trade Commission's Trade Regulation Rule entitled "Use of Negative Option Plans by Sellers in Commerce," 16 CFR Part 425.

(b) By taking action in this area:

(1) The Federal Trade Commission does not intend to preempt action in the same area, which is not inconsistent with this part, by any State, municipal, or other local government. This part does not annul or diminish any rights or remedies provided to consumers by any State law, municipal ordinance, or other local regulation, insofar as those rights or remedies are equal to or greater than those provided by this part. In addition, this part does not supersede those provisions of any State law, municipal ordinance, or other local regulation which impose obligations or liabilities upon sellers, when sellers subject to this part are not in compliance therewith.

(2) This part does supersede those provisions of any State law, municipal ordinance, or other local regulation which are inconsistent with this part to the extent that those provisions do not provide a buyer with rights which are equal to or greater than those rights granted a buyer by this part. This part also supersedes those provisions of any State law, municipal ordinance, or other local regula-

tion requiring that a buyer be notified of a right which is the same as a right provided by this part but requiring that a buyer be given notice of this right in a language, form, or manner which is different in any way from that required by this part. In those instances where any State law, municipal ordinance, or other local regulation contains provisions, some but not all of which are partially or completely superseded by this part, the provisions or portions of those provisions which have not been superseded retain their full force and effect.

(c) If any provision of this part, or its application to any person, partnership, corporation, act or practice is held invalid, the remainder of this part or the application of the provision to any other person, partnership, corporation, act or practice shall not be affected thereby.

SEC. 435.4 EFFECTIVE DATE OF THE RULE.

The original rule, which became effective 100 days after its promulgation on October 22, 1975, remains in effect. The amended rule, as set forth in this part, becomes effective March 1, 1994.

APPENDIX 6:
SAMPLE SELLER'S FIRST DELAY OPTION NOTICE (30 DAYS OR LESS)

Dear Customer:

We will be unable to ship the merchandise listed above until [date 30 days or less later than original promised time]. If you don't want to wait, you may cancel your order and receive a prompt refund by calling our toll-free customer service number, (800) 555-1234. If we do not hear from you before we ship the merchandise to you, we will assume that you have agreed to this shipment delay.

(Many merchants add clarifying language such as "Remember, if you *want* the merchandise, *don't* call.")*

---

*   Source: Federal Trade Commission.

APPENDIX 7:
SAMPLE SELLER'S FIRST DELAY OPTION NOTICE (INDEFINITE DELAY OF 30 DAYS OR MORE)

Dear Customer:

Because [explanation of backorder problem], we are unable to ship the merchandise listed above. We don't know when we will be able to ship it.

If you don't want to wait, you may cancel your order and receive a prompt refund by calling our toll-free customer service number, (800) 555-1234. If we do not hear from you and we have not shipped by [date 30 days later than original promised shipment time—in this example, 60 days after receipt of the properly completed order], your order will be cancelled automatically and your money will be refunded.

If you do not want your order automatically cancelled on [date 30 days later than original promised shipment time], you may request that we keep your order and fill it later. If you do request that we keep your order and fill it later, you still have the right to cancel the order at any time before we ship it to you. You may use our toll-free number, (800) 555-1234, either to request that we fill your order later or to cancel it.[1]

---

1   Source: Federal Trade Commission.

APPENDIX 8:
DIRECTORY OF ORGANIZATIONS WITH INFORMATION ON INTERNET INVESTMENTS

ORGANIZATION	ADDRESS	TELEPHONE NUMBER
Commodity Futures Trading Commission	Three Lafayette Centre, 1155 21st Street NW, Washington, DC 20581	202-418-5000
Federal Trade Commission	600 Pennsylvania Avenue NW, Washington, DC 20580	202-FTC-HELP (382-4357), 202-326-2502 (TDD)
National Association of Investors Corporation	PO Box 220, Royal Oak, MI 48068	248-583-6242
National Association of Securities Dealers	1735 K Street NW, Washington DC 20006-1500	202-728-8000
North American Securities Administrators Association Inc	.10 G Street NE, Suite 701, Washington, DC 20002	202-737-0900
Securities and Exchange Commission	450 Fifth Street NW, Washington, DC 20549	202-942-7040

Source: Federal Trade Commission.

APPENDIX 9:
DIRECTORY OF ORGANIZATIONS OFFERING ASSISTANCE AND INFORMATION ON INTERNET FRAUD

ORGANIZATION	ADDRESS	TELEPHONE NUMBER	WEBSITE	SERVICES PROVIDED
The American Express Company	801 Pennsylvania Avenue, NW, Washington, D.C. 20004	n/a	www.americanexpress.com	American Express offers a variety of tools to make online shopping safer including its smart card private payments and an online fraud protection guarantee, and provides a full description of website security, information collection and use, and how to decline email offers

ORGANIZATION	ADDRESS	TELEPHONE NUMBER	WEBSITE	SERVICES PROVIDED
Call For Action, Inc (CFA)	5272 River Road, Suite 300, Bethesda, Maryland 20816	301-657-8260	www.callforaction.org	CFA is an international, non-profit network of consumer hotlines affiliated with local broadcast partners.
The Consumer Information Center (CIC)	Pueblo, CO 81009	888-8-PUEBLO (888-878-3256)	www.pueblo.gsa.gov	The CIC publishes the Consumer Information Catalog which lists more than 200 publications from a variety of federal agencies
The Direct Marketing Association (DMA)	1111 19th Street NW, Suite 1100, Washington, D.C. 20036	n/a	www.the-dma.org	The DMA is a trade association of catalogers, financial services firms, publishers, book and music clubs, online service companies, and others involved in direct and database marketing and operates a Consumer Line which acts as an intermediary between consumers and companies to resolve complaints.

ORGANIZATION	ADDRESS	TELEPHONE NUMBER	WEBSITE	SERVICES PROVIDED
The Federal Trade Commission (FTC)	600 Pennsylvania Avenue NW, Washington, DC 20580	1-877-FTC-HELP (1-877-382-4357)	www.ftc.gov	The FTC works for the consumer to prevent fraudulent, deceptive and unfair business practices in the marketplace and to provide information to help consumers spot, stop and avoid them. The FTC hosts an on-line complaint for consumers who are victimized by fraudulent deceptive and unfair business practices, and enters internet, telemarketing, identity theft and other fraud-related complaints into Consumer Sentinel, a secure, online database available to hundreds of civil and criminal law enforcement agencies in the U.S. and abroad.

Source: American Express Company.

APPENDIX 10:
THE BETTER BUSINESS BUREAU CODE OF ONLINE BUSINESS PRACTICES

INTRODUCTION

1. The following Code of Online Business Practices is designed to guide ethical "business to customer" conduct in electronic commerce. These guidelines represent sound online advertising and selling practices that the Better Business Bureau ("BBB") and BBBOnLine believe will boost customer trust and confidence in online commerce.

2. This Code serves two purposes:

(a) First, the Code provides desirable standards for e-commerce generally. Adherence to the provisions of this Code will be a significant contribution toward effective self-regulation in the public interest. We urge online businesses to comply with the Code and to establish the necessary management procedures that will assure success.

(b) Second, it is the underpinning for the BBBOnLine Reliability Program and all Reliability participants must agree to follow it and to dispute resolution, at the customer's request, for unresolved disputes involving products or services advertised or purchased online. Online businesses that are or become Reliability participants will be able to demonstrate to the public their commitment to the Code's good business practices by displaying the Reliability Seal.

3. The Code contains practical, performance-based guidelines, rather than dictating methods for achieving the goals that could interfere with particular business models. While the Code establishes goals for the online business, it does not dictate how these goals should be reached, leaving those decisions up to the online business that knows its business model best. As such, the Code is designed to allow online businesses to take advantage of evolving technology and to foster innovation while adhering to principled business practices that provide truthful and accurate information to online customers.

4. The Code uses the term "should" in recognition that this is a voluntary code. However, all provisions are recommended for implementation by the online business community.

5. BBB and BBBOnLine encourage online businesses, to the extent they target particular geographic markets or countries with their online advertising or marketing, to consider the targeted geographical markets' or countries' regulatory requirements. However, the Code does not address whether the laws, if any, of any particular jurisdiction apply to online advertising or transactions. Online businesses are therefore advised to make a determination that their practices are in compliance with applicable laws.

6. E-commerce is developing at a rapid pace and BBB and BBBOnLine recognize that this Code may need to be modified over time to keep it current with developing technology, new business models, and customer needs. BBB and BBBOnLine are committed to review the Code and update it as needed.

7. Terms:

(a) Online Advertiser: A person or entity acts as an "online advertiser" when it promotes its own goods or services on the Internet. Therefore, code provisions referring to online advertisers apply when the business is acting as an online advertiser for a particular activity. If in certain situations an online advertiser acts as an online merchant, then in those situations, it must also comply with the online merchant Code requirements.

(b) Online Merchant: A person or entity acts as an "online merchant" when it offers its own goods and services online and accepts online orders. A business may act as an online merchant in certain situations but not in others. Therefore, Code provisions referring to online merchants apply when the business is acting as an online merchant for a particular activity. All online merchants are also online advertisers and as such, should adhere to online advertiser Code provisions as well.

(c) Purchase: For purposes of this Code, the term "purchase" is intended to be used broadly and is meant to include other transactions, including but not limited to, leasing, licensing or barter.

PRINCIPLES FOR ETHICAL BUSINESS TO CUSTOMER CONDUCT

The following statements represent the five principles upon which this Code is based.

Principle I: Truthful and Accurate Communication

Online advertisers should not engage in deceptive or misleading trade practices with regard to any aspect of electronic commerce, including advertising, marketing, or in their use of technology.

A. Online advertisers should adhere to the Better Business Bureau's Code of Advertising. Online advertisers should engage in truthful advertising. They should not make deceptive or misleading representations or omissions of material facts.

1. Online advertisers should be able to substantiate any express or reasonably implied factual claims made in their advertising or marketing and should possess reasonable substantiation prior to disseminating a claim.

2. Online advertisers should disclose their advertising or marketing to be such if failure to do so would be misleading.

(a) For example, if material information in an advertisement appears misleading because it is difficult to distinguish between editorial content and advertising, the advertising should be labeled as such.

(b) Likewise, online advertisers should not disguise advertising as technical or desktop functionality when doing so would mislead customers into clicking on the advertisement thinking that they were actually performing a technical function.

3. If online advertisers make price comparisons, they should disclose the basis for, or the geographic area that constitutes, the market area. In all cases, online advertisers should either disclose the date when the comparison was made or if they offer ongoing claims, keep the substantiation current.

4. Online advertisers should cooperate with any bona fide, industry self-regulatory advertising programs where such programs exist to resolve any advertising disputes.

B. Online advertisers should use Internet technology to promote the customer's knowledge of the products or services being offered and should not use technology to mislead customers.

1. Online advertisers should not mislead online customers by creating the false impression of sponsorship, endorsement, popularity, trustworthiness, product quality or business size through the misuse of hyperlinks, "seals", other technology, or another's intellectual property.

2. Online advertisers may use hyperlinks to add to or supplement information about goods or services but should not misleadingly use hyperlinks or information provided via a hyperlink to:

(a) contradict or substantially change the meaning of any material statement or claim;

(b) create the false impression of affiliation;

(c) create the false impression that the content, merchandise or service of another's business is their own.

3. Online advertisers should only use search terms or mechanisms that fairly reflect the content of their site.

4. Online advertisers should make sure that any third-party "seals" or endorsements that incorporate links to self-regulatory or ethical standard programs are functional so that customers can easily verify membership in the seal program and determine its purpose, scope, and standards. Any online advertiser that participates in any third-party self-regulatory or ethical standard or seal program should do so in conformity with that program's instructions regarding the display, activation, and uses of the seal or endorsement. If an express or implied claim is made through the use of a seal or text, the online advertiser should provide customers with the opportunity to understand the details behind the program, including the program's claims, scope and standards.

5. Online advertisers should not knowingly link to, or accept affinity or royalty payments from, deceptive, fraudulent, or illegal sites.

6. Online advertisers should not deceptively interfere with a customer's browser, computer, or any appliance the customer uses to access the Internet.

Principle II: Disclosure

Online merchants should disclose to their customers and prospective customers information about the business, the goods or services available for purchase online, and the transaction itself.

A. All information required by this Code should meet the following standards:

1. It should be clear, accurate, and easy to find and understand;

2. It should be readily accessible online and can appear via a noticeable and descriptive hyperlink or other similarly effective mechanism;

3. It should be presented such that customers can access and maintain an adequate record of it;

4. And, if the information relates to the goods or services available for purchase online or the transaction itself, it should be accessible prior to the consummation of the transaction.

B. Information About the Business:

1. Online merchants should provide, at a minimum, the following contact information online:

(a) legal name;

(b) the name under which it conducts business;

(c) the principle physical address or information, including country, sufficient to ensure the customer can locate the business offline;

(d) an online method of contact such as e-mail;

(e) a point of contact within the organization that is responsible for customer inquires; and

(f) a telephone number unless to do so would be disruptive to the operation of the business given its size and resources and then, the merchant should maintain a working listed phone number.

2. Online merchants that register an Internet domain name should provide complete and accurate information to the authorized Internet registrar with which they register and should use the appropriate top-level domain for the type of business registered.

C. Information About Goods and Services Available for Purchase Online: Online merchants should provide enough information available about the goods or services available online so that customers can make an informed choice about whether to purchase such goods or services.

D. Information About the Online Transaction Itself: 10 Online merchants should provide enough information about the online transaction itself so that customers can make an informed choice about whether to engage in the online transaction.

1. Online merchants should disclose material information about the online transaction itself including, but not limited to:

(a) terms of the transaction

(b) product availability/shipping information; and

(c) prices and customer costs.

2. And should provide the customer with an opportunity to:

(a) review and approve the transaction and

(b) receive a confirmation.

3. If the online merchant chooses to provide some information in more than one language, all material information about the transaction should be available in the selected languages. Similarly, if the online merchant chooses to reach a particular population, such as the aged or handicapped, by using large font sizes or specific colors for example, all material information about the transaction should be provided in the same way.

E. Terms of the Online Transaction: Online merchants should provide the terms of the online transaction including but not limited to:

1. Any restrictions or limitations (for example, time or geographic) they impose on the sale of the goods or services;

2. Easy-to-use payment mechanisms;

3. Return or refund policies, including how customers can make returns or exchanges; obtain refunds or credits; or cancel a transaction; and any associated time limitations or associated fees;.

4. For products, any warrantees, guarantees, escrow programs or other offered terms, including limitations, conditions, if any;

5. For services, any material standards, schedules, fees, or other offered terms, including limitation and conditions;

6. For contests, sweepstakes or other similar promotions, the complete rules adjacent to, or in a hyperlink or similar technology adjacent to, the promotion itself; and

7. For ongoing transactions or subscriptions:

(a) information about how the transaction will appear on the bill so that the customer can easily identify the business and the transaction on the bill;

(b) easy-to-understand cancellation information, an easy to use means to cancel an ongoing subscription, and timely confirmation of such cancellation.

F. Product Availability/Terms of Shipping: Online merchants should:

1. Note which products or services are temporarily unavailable and in those instances:

(a) provide information about when the customer will be charged for the transaction; and

(b) if an expected availability date is provided for unavailable products or services, have a reasonable basis for such date.

2. Have a reasonable basis for, and provide customers with, estimated shipping times (or in the case of online delivery, delivery times) (if such times are unknown at the time of the online transaction, the online merchant should provide the information via a timely follow-up e-mail but should provide the customer with the opportunity to cancel the transaction if the time indicated is unacceptable);

3. Have a reasonable basis for stated delivery claims when made;

4. Disclose any shipping, performance, or delivery limitations they impose (age, geographic); and

5. If a material delay in shipping or performance occurs, provide the customer with timely information about the delay and the opportunity to cancel the transaction.

G. Prices and Customer Costs: Online merchants should:

1. Disclose, in a specified currency, an itemized list of the prices or fees and expected customer costs to be collected by the online merchant with regard to an online transaction, including but not limited to:

(a) price or license fee to be charged, or in the case of a barter trade, the items that will be exchanged for goods or services purchased or licensed;

(b) expected shipping and handling charges (if such charges are unknown at the time of the online transaction, the online merchant should provide the information via a timely follow-up e-mail but should provide the customer with the opportunity to cancel the transaction if the costs are unacceptable); and

(c) expected taxes or other government imposed fees collected by the online merchant related to the transaction, etc.;

2. Provide a generalized description of other routine costs and fees related to the transaction that may be incurred by the customer such as tariffs or routine subscription fees that may not be collected by the online merchant;

3. Clearly identify the merchant's name and website address on any subsequent statements or other billing information; and

4. Honor the amount authorized by the customer in any subsequent bills to the customer.

H. Provide Opportunity to Review and Approve Transaction Prior to completion of the transaction, online merchants should provide customers with the option to review the online transaction and to confirm their intent to enter into the transaction by providing a summary that includes:

1. Information about the online transaction (as outlined in sections above);

2. The selected payment method; and

3. The option to cancel or affirmatively complete the transaction.

I. Provide Confirmation of the Sale: Online merchants should provide customers with the option to receive a confirmation of the transaction after the transaction has been completed. The confirmation should include:

1. A line-itemed statement of what was ordered, the price, and any other known charges such as shipping/handling and taxes,

2. Sufficient contact information to enable purchasers to obtain order status updates, and

3. The anticipated date of shipment. Online merchants should disclose to their customers and prospective customers information about the business, the goods or services available for purchase online, and the transaction itself.

Principle III: Information Practices and Security

Online advertisers should adopt information practices that treat customers' personal information with care. They should post and adhere to a privacy policy based on fair information principles, take appropriate measures to provide adequate security, and respect customers' preferences regarding unsolicited email.

A. Post and Adhere to a Privacy Policy Online advertisers should post and adhere to a privacy policy that is open, transparent, and meets generally accepted fair information principles including providing notice as to what personal information the online advertiser collects, uses, and discloses; what choices customers have with regard to the business' collection, use and, disclosure of that information; what access customers have to the information; what security measures are taken to protect the information, and what enforcement and redress mechanisms are in place to remedy any violations of the policy. The privacy policy should be easy to find and understand and be available prior to or at the time the customer provides any personally identifiable information.

B. Provide Adequate Security Online advertisers should use appropriate levels of security for the type of information collected, maintained, or transferred to third parties and should:

1. Use industry standard levels of encryption and authentication for the transfer or receipt of health care information, social security numbers, financial transaction information (for example, a credit card number), or other sensitive information;

2. Provide industry standard levels of security and integrity to protect data being maintained by computers; and

3. Take reasonable steps to require third parties involved in fulfilling a customer transaction to also maintain appropriate levels of security.

C. Respect Customer's Preferences Regarding Unsolicited E-mail: Online advertisers should accurately describe their business practices with regard to their use of unsolicited e-mail to customers.

1. Online advertisers that engage in unsolicited email marketing should post and adhere to a "Do Not Contact" policy—a policy that, at a minimum, enables those customers who do not wish to be contacted online to "opt out" online from future solicitations. This policy should be available both on the website and in any emails, other than those relating to a particular order.

2. Online advertisers that engage in unsolicited email marketing should also subscribe to a bona-fide e-mail suppression list such as ones offered by Center for Democracy and Technology at http://opt-out.cdt.org and the Direct Marketing Association at http://www.e-mps.org/en.

Principle IV: Customer Satisfaction

Online merchants should seek to ensure their customers are satisfied by honoring their representations, answering questions, and resolving customer complaints and disputes in a timely and responsive manner.

A. Honor Representations: Online merchants should comply with all commitments, representations, and other promises made to a customer.

B. Answer Questions: Online merchants should provide an easy-to-find and understand notice of how customers can successfully and meaningfully contact the business to get answers to their questions. Online merchants should promptly and substantively respond to the customer's commercially reasonable questions.

C. Resolve Customer Complaints and Disputes: Online merchants should seek to resolve customer complaints and disputes in a fair, timely, and effective manner.

1. Online merchants should provide an easy-to-find and understandable notice of how a customer can successfully and meaningfully contact the business to expeditiously resolve complaints and disputes related to a transaction.

2. Online merchants shall have an effective and easy to use internal mechanism for addressing complaints and correcting errors. Examples include fair exchange policies, return policies, etc.

3. In the event the customer's complaint cannot be resolved, online merchants shall also offer a fair method for resolving differences with regard to a transaction by offering either an unconditional money-back guarantee or third-party dispute resolution.

(a) If an online merchant offers third party dispute resolution, it should use a trusted third party that offers impartial, accessible, and timely arbitration that is free to consumers or at a charge to consumers that is not disproportionate to the value of goods or services involved in the dispute.

(b) Online merchants should provide customers with easy-to-find and understandable contact information for such third parties, including a link (or similar technology) to any third party sites used for such means.

Principle V: Protecting Children

If online advertisers target children under the age of 13, they should take special care to protect children by recognizing their developing cognitive abilities.

A. Online advertisers should adhere to the Children's Advertising Review Unit's ("CARU) Self Regulatory Guidelines for Children's Advertising.

B. Specifically, online advertisers should adhere to the Guidelines for Interactive Electronic Media that apply to online activities, which are intentionally targeted to children under 13, or where the website knows the visitor is a child. These Guidelines include parental permission first requirements in the "Making a Sale" and "Data Collection" provisions. Online advertisers should not engage in deceptive or misleading trade practices with regard to any aspect of electronic commerce, including advertising, marketing, or in their use of technology.

A. Online advertisers should adhere to the Better Business Bureau's Code of Advertising. Online advertisers should engage in truthful advertising. They should not make deceptive or misleading representations or omissions of material facts.

1. Online advertisers should be able to substantiate any express or reasonably implied factual claims made in their advertising or marketing and should possess reasonable substantiation prior to disseminating a claim.

2. Online advertisers should disclose their advertising or marketing to be such if failure to do so would be misleading.

(a) For example, if material information in an advertisement appears misleading because it is difficult to distinguish between editorial content and advertising, the advertising should be labeled as such.

(b) Likewise, online advertisers should not disguise advertising as technical or desktop functionality when doing so would mislead customers into clicking on the advertisement thinking that they were actually performing a technical function.

3. If online advertisers make price comparisons, they should disclose the basis for, or the geographic area that constitutes, the market area. In all cases, online advertisers should either disclose the date when the comparison was made or if they offer ongoing claims, keep the substantiation current.

4. Online advertisers should cooperate with any bona fide, industry self-regulatory advertising programs where such programs exist to resolve any advertising disputes.

B. Online advertisers should use Internet technology to promote the customer's knowledge of the products or services being offered and should not use technology to mislead customers.

1. Online advertisers should not mislead online customers by creating the false impression of sponsorship, endorsement, popularity, trustworthiness, product quality or business size through the misuse of hyperlinks, "seals", other technology, or another's intellectual property.

2. Online advertisers may use hyperlinks to add to or supplement information about goods or services but should not misleadingly use hyperlinks or information provided via a hyperlink to:

(a) contradict or substantially change the meaning of any material statement or claim;

(b) create the false impression of affiliation;

(c) create the false impression that the content, merchandise or service of another's business is their own.

3. Online advertisers should only use search terms or mechanisms that fairly reflect the content of their site.

4. Online advertisers should make sure that any third-party "seals" or endorsements that incorporate links to self-regulatory or ethical standard programs are functional so that customers can easily verify membership in the seal program and determine its purpose, scope, and standards. Any online advertiser that participates in any third-party self-regulatory or ethical standard or seal program should do so in conformity with that program's instructions regarding the display, activation, and uses of the seal or endorsement. If an express or implied claim is made through the use of a seal or text, the online advertiser should provide customers with the opportunity to understand the details behind the program, including the program's claims, scope and standards.

5. Online advertisers should not knowingly link to, or accept affinity or royalty payments from, deceptive, fraudulent, or illegal sites.

6. Online advertisers should not deceptively interfere with a customer's browser, computer, or any appliance the customer uses to access the Internet.

Source: Better Business Bureau.

APPENDIX 11:
THE CHILDREN'S ONLINE PRIVACY
PROTECTION ACT OF 1998

SEC. 1301. SHORT TITLE.

This title may be cited as the "Children's Online Privacy Protection Act of 1998".

SEC. 1302. DEFINITIONS.

In this title:

(1) CHILD.—The term "child" means an individual under the age of 13.

(2) OPERATOR.—The term "operator"—

(A) means any person who operates a website located on the Internet or an online service and who collects or maintains personal information from or about the users of or visitors to such website or online service, or on whose behalf such information is collected or maintained, where such website or online service is operated for commercial purposes, including any person offering products or services for sale through that website or online service, involving commerce—

(i) among the several States or with 1 or more foreign nations;

(ii) in any territory of the United States or in the District of Columbia, or between any such territory and—

(I) another such territory; or

(II) any State or foreign nation; or

(iii) between the District of Columbia and any State, territory, or foreign nation; but

(B) does not include any nonprofit entity that would otherwise be exempt from coverage under section 5 of the Federal Trade Commission Act (15 U.S.C. 45).

(3) COMMISSION.—The term "Commission" means the Federal Trade Commission.

(4) DISCLOSURE.—The term "disclosure" means, with respect to personal information—

(A) the release of personal information collected from a child in identifiable form by an operator for any purpose, except where such information is provided to a person other than the operator who provides support for the internal operations of the website and does not disclose or use that information for any other purpose; and

(B) making personal information collected from a child by a website or online service directed to children or with actual knowledge that such information was collected from a child, publicly available in identifiable form, by any means including by a public posting, through the Internet, or through—

(i) a home page of a website;

(ii) a pen pal service;

(iii) an electronic mail service;

(iv) a message board; or

(v) a chat room.

(5) FEDERAL AGENCY.—The term "Federal agency" means an agency, as that term is defined in section 551(1) of title 5, United States Code.

(6) INTERNET.—The term "Internet" means collectively the myriad of computer and telecommunications facilities, including equipment and operating software, which comprise the interconnected world-wide network of networks that employ the Transmission Control Protocol/ Internet Protocol, or any predecessor or successor protocols to such protocol, to communicate information of all kinds by wire or radio.

(7) PARENT.—The term "parent" includes a legal guardian.

(8) PERSONAL INFORMATION.—The term "personal information" means individually identifiable information about an individual collected online, including—

(A) a first and last name;

(B) a home or other physical address including street name and name of a city or town;

(C) an e-mail address;

(D) a telephone number;

(E) a Social Security number;

(F) any other identifier that the Commission determines permits the physical or online contacting of a specific individual; or

(G) information concerning the child or the parents of that child that the website collects online from the child and combines with an identifier described in this paragraph.

(9) VERIFIABLE PARENTAL CONSENT.—The term "verifiable parental consent" means any reasonable effort (taking into consideration available technology), including a request for authorization for future collection, use, and disclosure described in the notice, to ensure that a parent of a child receives notice of the operator's personal information collection, use, and disclosure practices, and authorizes the collection, use, and disclosure, as applicable, of personal information and the subsequent use of that information before that information is collected from that child.

(10) WEBSITE OR ONLINE SERVICE DIRECTED TO CHILDREN.—

(A) IN GENERAL.—The term "website or online service directed to children" means—

(i) a commercial website or online service that is targeted to children; or

(ii) that portion of a commercial website or online service that is targeted to children.

(B) LIMITATION.—A commercial website or online service, or a portion of a commercial website or online service, shall not be deemed directed to children solely for referring or linking to a commercial website or online service directed to children by using information location tools, including a directory, index, reference, pointer, or hypertext link.

(11) PERSON.—The term "person" means any individual, partnership, corporation, trust, estate, cooperative, association, or other entity.

(12) ONLINE CONTACT INFORMATION.—The term "online contact information" means an e-mail address or an-other substantially similar identifier that permits direct contact with a person online.

SEC. 1303. REGULATION OF UNFAIR AND DECEPTIVE ACTS AND PRACTICES IN CONNECTION WITH THE COLLECTION AND USE OF PERSONAL INFORMATION FROM AND ABOUT CHILDREN ON THE INTERNET.

(a) ACTS PROHIBITED.—

(1) IN GENERAL.—It is unlawful for an operator of a website or online service directed to children, or any operator that has actual knowledge that it is collecting personal information from a child, to collect personal information from a child in a manner that violates the regulations prescribed under subsection (b).

(2) DISCLOSURE TO PARENT PROTECTED.—Notwithstanding paragraph (1), neither an operator of such a website or online service nor the operator's agent shall be held to be liable under any Federal or State law for any disclosure made in good faith and following reasonable procedures in responding to a request for disclosure of personal information under subsection (b)(1)(B)(iii) to the parent of a child.

(b) REGULATIONS.—

(1) IN GENERAL.—Not later than 1 year after the date of the enactment of this Act, the Commission shall promulgate under section 553 of title 5, United States Code, regulations that—

(A) require the operator of any website or online service directed to children that collects personal information from children or the operator of a website or online service that has actual knowledge that it is collecting personal information from a child—

(i) to provide notice on the website of what information is collected from children by the operator, how the operator uses such information, and the operator's disclosure practices for such information; and

(ii) to obtain verifiable parental consent for the collection, use, or disclosure of personal information from children;

(B) require the operator to provide, upon request of a parent under this subparagraph whose child has provided personal information to that website or online service, upon proper identification of that parent, to such parent—

(i) a description of the specific types of personal information collected from the child by that operator;

(ii) the opportunity at any time to refuse to permit the operator's further use or maintenance in retrievable form, or future online collection, of personal information from that child; and

(iii) notwithstanding any other provision of law, a means that is reasonable under the circumstances for the parent to obtain any personal information collected from that child;

(C) prohibit conditioning a child's participation in a game, the offering of a prize, or another activity on the child disclosing more personal information than is reasonably necessary to participate in such activity; and

(D) require the operator of such a website or online service to establish and maintain reasonable procedures to protect the confidentiality, security, and integrity of personal information collected from children.

(2) WHEN CONSENT NOT REQUIRED.—The regulations shall provide that verifiable parental consent under paragraph (1)(A)(ii) is not required in the case of—

(A) online contact information collected from a child that is used only to respond directly on a one-time basis to a specific request from the child and is not used to recontact the child and is not maintained in retrievable form by the operator;

(B) a request for the name or online contact information of a parent or child that is used for the sole purpose of obtaining parental consent or providing notice under this section and where such information is not maintained in retrievable form by the operator if parental consent is not obtained after a reasonable time;

(C) online contact information collected from a child that is used only to respond more than once directly to a specific request from the child and is not used to recontact the child beyond the scope of that request—

(i) if, before any additional response after the initial response to the child, the operator uses reasonable efforts to provide a parent notice of the online contact information collected from the child, the purposes for which it is to be used, and an opportunity for the parent to request that the operator make no further use of the information and that it not be maintained in retrievable form; or

(ii) without notice to the parent in such circumstances as the Commission may determine are appropriate, taking into consideration the benefits to the child of access to information and services, and risks to the security and privacy of the child, in regulations promulgated under this subsection;

(D) the name of the child and online contact information (to the extent reasonably necessary to protect the safety of a child participant on the site)—

(i) used only for the purpose of protecting such safety;

(ii) not used to recontact the child or for any other purpose; and

(iii) not disclosed on the site, if the operator uses reasonable efforts to provide a parent notice of the name and online contact information collected from the child, the purposes for which it is to be used, and an opportunity for the parent to request that the operator make no further use of the information and that it not be maintained in retrievable form; or

(E) the collection, use, or dissemination of such information by the operator of such a website or online service necessary—

(i) to protect the security or integrity of its website;

(ii) to take precautions against liability;

(iii) to respond to judicial process; or

(iv) to the extent permitted under other provisions of law, to provide information to law enforcement agencies or for an investigation on a matter related to public safety. 1815

(3) TERMINATION OF SERVICE.—The regulations shall permit the operator of a website or an online service to terminate service provided to a child whose parent has refused, under the regulations prescribed under paragraph (1)(B)(ii), to permit the operator's further use or maintenance in retrievable form, or future online collection, of personal information from that child.

(c) ENFORCEMENT.—Subject to sections 1304 and 1306, a violation of a regulation prescribed under subsection (a) shall be treated as a violation of a rule defining an unfair or deceptive act or practice prescribed under section 18(a)(1)(B) of the Federal Trade Commission Act (15 U.S.C. 57a(a)(1)(B)).

(d) INCONSISTENT STATE LAW.—No State or local government may impose any liability for commercial activities or actions by operators in interstate or foreign commerce in connection with an activity or action described in this title that is inconsistent with the treatment of those activities or actions under this section.

SEC. 1304. SAFE HARBORS.

(a) GUIDELINES.—An operator may satisfy the requirements of regulations issued under section 1303(b) by following a set of self-regulatory guidelines, issued by representatives of the marketing or online industries, or by other persons, approved under subsection (b).

(b) INCENTIVES.—

(1) SELF-REGULATORY INCENTIVES.—In prescribing regulations under section 1303, the Commission shall provide incentives for self-regulation by operators to implement the protections afforded children under the regulatory requirements described in subsection (b) of that section.

(2) DEEMED COMPLIANCE.—Such incentives shall include provisions for ensuring that a person will be deemed to be in compliance with the requirements of the regulations under section 1303 if that person complies with guidelines that, after notice and comment, are approved by the Commission upon making a determination that the guidelines meet the requirements of the regulations issued under section 1303.

(3) EXPEDITED RESPONSE TO REQUESTS.—The Commission shall act upon requests for safe harbor treatment within 180 days of the filing of the request, and shall set forth in writing its conclusions with regard to such requests.

(c) APPEALS.—Final action by the Commission on a request for approval of guidelines, or the failure to act within 180 days on a request for approval of guidelines, submitted under subsection (b) may be appealed to a district court of the United States of appropriate jurisdiction as provided for in section 706 of title 5, United States Code.

SEC. 1305. ACTIONS BY STATES.

(a) IN GENERAL.—

(1) CIVIL ACTIONS.—In any case in which the attorney general of a State has reason to believe that an interest of the residents of that State has been or is threatened or adversely affected by the engagement of any person in a practice that violates any regulation of the Commission prescribed under section 1303(b), the State, as parens patriae, may bring a civil action on behalf of the residents of the State in a district court of the United States of appropriate jurisdiction to—

(A) enjoin that practice;

(B) enforce compliance with the regulation;

(C) obtain damage, restitution, or other compensation on behalf of residents of the State; or

(D) obtain such other relief as the court may consider to be appropriate.

(2) NOTICE.—

(A) IN GENERAL.—Before filing an action under paragraph (1), the attorney general of the State involved shall provide to the Commission—

(i) written notice of that action; and

(ii) a copy of the complaint for that action.

(B) EXEMPTION.—

(i) IN GENERAL.—Subparagraph (A) shall not apply with respect to the filing of an action by an attorney general of a State under this subsection, if the attorney general determines that it is not feasible to provide the notice described in that subparagraph before the filing of the action.

(ii) NOTIFICATION.—In an action described in clause (i), the attorney general of a State shall provide notice and a copy of the complaint to the Commission at the same time as the attorney general files the action.

(b) INTERVENTION.—

(1) IN GENERAL.—On receiving notice under subsection (a)(2), the Commission shall have the right to intervene in the action that is the subject of the notice.

(2) EFFECT OF INTERVENTION.—If the Commission intervenes in an action under subsection (a), it shall have the right—

(A) to be heard with respect to any matter that arises in that action; and

(B) to file a petition for appeal.

(3) AMICUS CURIAE.—Upon application to the court, a person whose self-regulatory guidelines have been approved by the Commission and are relied upon as a defense by any defendant to a proceeding under this section may file amicus curiae in that proceeding.

(c) CONSTRUCTION.—For purposes of bringing any civil action under subsection (a), nothing in this title shall be construed to prevent an attorney general of a State from exercising the powers conferred on the attorney general by the laws of that State to—

(1) conduct investigations;

(2) administer oaths or affirmations; or

(3) compel the attendance of witnesses or the production of documentary and other evidence.

(d) ACTIONS BY THE COMMISSION.—In any case in which an action is instituted by or on behalf of the Commission for violation of any regulation prescribed under section 1303, no State may, during the pendency of that action, institute an action under subsection (a) against any defendant named in the complaint in that action for violation of that regulation.

(e) VENUE; SERVICE OF PROCESS.—

(1) VENUE.—Any action brought under subsection (a) may be brought in the district court of the United States that meets applicable requirements relating to venue under section 1391 of title 28, United States Code.

(2) SERVICE OF PROCESS.—In an action brought under subsection (a), process may be served in any district in which the defendant—

(A) is an inhabitant; or

(B) may be found.

SEC. 1306. ADMINISTRATION AND APPLICABILITY OF ACT.

(a) IN GENERAL.—Except as otherwise provided, this title shall be enforced by the Commission under the Federal Trade Commission Act (15 U.S.C. 41 et seq.).

(b) PROVISIONS.—Compliance with the requirements imposed under this title shall be enforced under—

(1) section 8 of the Federal Deposit Insurance Act (12 U.S.C. 1818), in the case of—

(A) national banks, and Federal branches and Federal agencies of foreign banks, by the Office of the Comptroller of the Currency;

(B) member banks of the Federal Reserve System (other than national banks), branches and agencies of foreign banks (other than Federal branches, Federal agencies, and insured State branches of foreign banks), commercial lending companies owned or controlled by foreign banks, and organizations operating under section 25 or

25(a) of the Federal Reserve Act (12 U.S.C. 601 et seq. and 611 et seq.), by the Board; and

(C) banks insured by the Federal Deposit Insurance Corporation (other than members of the Federal Reserve System) and insured State branches of foreign banks, by the Board of Direc- tors of the Federal Deposit Insurance Corporation;

(2) section 8 of the Federal Deposit Insurance Act (12 U.S.C. 1818), by the Director of the Office of Thrift Supervision, in the case of a savings association the deposits of which are insured by the Federal Deposit Insurance Corporation;

(3) the Federal Credit Union Act (12 U.S.C. 1751 et seq.) by the National Credit Union Administration Board with respect to any Federal credit union;

(4) part A of subtitle VII of title 49, United States Code, by the Secretary of Transportation with respect to any air carrier or foreign air carrier subject to that part;

(5) the Packers and Stockyards Act, 1921 (7 U.S.C. 181 et seq.) (except as provided in section 406 of that Act (7 U.S.C. 226, 227)), by the Secretary of Agriculture with respect to any activities subject to that Act; and

(6) the Farm Credit Act of 1971 (12 U.S.C. 2001 et seq.) by the Farm Credit Administration with respect to any Federal land bank, Federal land bank association, Federal intermediate credit bank, or production credit association.

(c) EXERCISE OF CERTAIN POWERS.—For the purpose of the exercise by any agency referred to in subsection (a) of its powers under any Act referred to in that subsection, a violation of any requirement imposed under this title shall be deemed to be a violation of a requirement imposed under that Act. In addition to its powers under any provision of law specifically referred to in subsection (a), each of the agencies referred to in that subsection may exercise, for the purpose of enforcing compliance with any requirement imposed under this title, any other authority conferred on it by law.

(d) ACTIONS BY THE COMMISSION.—The Commission shall prevent any person from violating a rule of the Commission under section 1303 in the same manner, by the same means, and with the same jurisdiction, powers, and duties as though all applicable terms and provisions of the Federal Trade Commission Act (15 U.S.C. 41 et seq.) were incorporated into and made a part of this title. Any entity that violates such rule shall be subject to the penalties and entitled to the privileges and immunities provided in the Federal Trade Commission Act in the same manner, by the same means, and with the same jurisdiction, power, and duties as though all applicable terms and provisions of the Federal Trade Commission Act were incorporated into and made a part of this title.

(e) EFFECT ON OTHER LAWS.—Nothing contained in the Act shall be construed to limit the authority of the Commission under any other provisions of law.

SEC. 1307. REVIEW.

Not later than 5 years after the effective date of the regulations initially issued under section 1303, the Commission shall—

(1) review the implementation of this title, including the effect of the implementation of this title on practices relating to the collection and disclosure of information relating to children, children's ability to obtain access to information of their choice online, and on the availability of websites directed to children; and

(2) prepare and submit to Congress a report on the results of the review under paragraph (1).

SEC. 1308. EFFECTIVE DATE.

Sections 1303(a), 1305, and 1306 of this title take effect on the later of—

(1) the date that is 18 months after the date of enactment of this Act; or

(2) the date on which the Commission rules on the first application filed for safe harbor treatment under section 1304 if the Commission does not rule on the first such application within one year after the date of enactment of this Act, but in no case later than the date that is 30 months after the date of enactment of this Act.

APPENDIX 12:
GOVERNMENTS WHICH HAVE SIGNED ONTO THE INTERNATIONAL GUIDELINES FOR INTERNET SHOPPING IN THE INTERNATIONAL MARKETPLACE

Australia

Austria

Belgium

Canada

Czech Republic

Denmark

Finland

France

Germany

Greece

Hungary

Iceland

Ireland

Italy

Japan

Korea

Luxembourg

Mexico

The Netherlands

New Zealand

Norway

Poland

Portugal

Spain

Sweden

Switzerland

Turkey

United Kingdom

United States

Source: Federal Trade Commission.

GLOSSARY

Acceleration Clause—An acceleration clause is a provision or clause in a contract or document establishing that upon the occurrence of a certain event, such as a default in payments, a party's expected interest in the subject property will become prematurely vested.

Acceptance—Acceptance refers to one's consent to the terms of an offer, which consent creates a contract.

Accord and Satisfaction—Accord and satisfaction refers to the payment of money, or other thing of value, which is usually less than the amount owed or demanded, in exchange for extinguishment of the debt.

Actual Damages—Actual damages are those damages directly referable to the breach or tortious act and which can be readily proven to have been sustained and for which the injured party should be compensated as a matter of right. Also referred to as compensatory or general damages.

Adhesion Contract—An adhesion contract is a standardized contract form offered to consumers of goods and services on a "take it or leave it" basis without affording the consumer a realistic opportunity to bargain, and under such conditions that the consumer cannot obtain the desired product or service except by acquiescing in form contract.

Agency—Agency is the relationship in which one person acts for or represents another by the latter's authority, such as principal and agent or proprietor and independent contractor relationships.

Agent—An agent is one who represents and acts for another under the contract or relation of agency.

Amortization Schedule—An amortization schedule is a plan for the payment of an indebtedness where there are partial payments of the principal and accrued interest, at stated periods for a definite time, upon the expiration of which the entire indebtedness will be extinguished.

Annual Percentage Rate (APR)—The annual percentage rate is the actual cost of borrowing money, expressed in the form of an annual rate to make it easy for one to compare the cost of borrowing money among several lenders.

Anticipatory Breach—An anticipatory breach is one a breach committed prior to the actual time of required performance which occurs when one party by declaration repudiates his contractual obligation before it is due.

Apparent Agency—Apparent agency refers to the situation when one person, whether or not authorized, reasonably appears to a third person, due to the manifestation of another, to be authorized to act as agent for such other.

Attorney In Fact—An attorney-in-fact is an agent or representative of another given authority to act in that person's name and place pursuant to a document called a "power of attorney."

Bankrupt—Bankrupt refers to the state or condition of one who is unable to pay his debts as they are, or become, due.

Bankruptcy—Bankruptcy is the legal process under federal law intended to insure fairness and equality among creditors of a bankrupt person, also known as a debtor, and to enable the debtor to start fresh by retaining certain property exempt from liabilities and unhampered by preexisting debts.

Bilateral Contract—A bilateral contract is one containing mutual promises between the parties to the contract, each being termed both a promisor and a promisee.

Boilerplate—Boilerplate refers to the standard or formal language found in legal documents of a given type, often in small print.

Bookmark—A bookmark is an online function that lets the user access their favorite web sites quickly.

Breach of Contract—A breach of contract refers to the failure, without any legal excuse, to perform any promise which forms the whole or the part of a contract.

Browser—A browser is special software that allows the user to navigate several areas of the internet and view a website.

Bulletin Board—A bulletin board is a place to leave an electronic message or share news to which anyone can read and reply.

Capacity—Capacity is the legal qualification concerning the ability of one to understand the nature and effects of one's acts.

Chat Room—A chat room is a place for people to converse online by typing messages to each other.

Chatting—Chatting is a way for a group of people to converse online in real-time by typing messages to each other.

Collateral—Collateral is property which is pledged as security for the satisfaction of a debt.

Common Law—Common law is the system of jurisprudence which originated in England and was later applied in the United States. The common law is based on judicial precedent rather than statutory law.

Compensatory Damages—Compensatory damages are those damages directly referable to the breach or tortious act and which can be readily proven to have been sustained and for which the injured party should be compensated as a matter of right. Also referred to as actual or general damages.

Condition—A condition is a future and uncertain event upon the happening of which is made to depend the existence of an obligation.

Condition Concurrent—A condition concurrent is a condition precedent which exists only when parties to a contract are found to render performance at the same time.

Condition Precedent—A condition precedent is a condition which must occur before the agreement becomes effective and which calls for the happening of some event before the contract shall be binding on the parties.

Condition Subsequent—A condition subsequent is a provision giving one party the right to divest himself of liability and obligation to perform further if the other party fails to meet the condition.

Consequential Damages—Consequential damages are those damages which are caused by an injury but which are not a necessary result of the injury and must be specially pleaded and proven in order to be awarded.

Consideration—Consideration is something of value given in return for a performance or promise of performance by another, for the purpose of forming a contract.

Contract—A contract is an agreement between two or more persons which creates an obligation to do or not to do a particular thing.

Cookie—When the user visits a site, a notation may be fed to a file known as a "cookie" in their computer for future reference. If the user revisits the site, the "cookie" file allows the web site to identify the user as a "return" guest and offers the user products tailored to their interests or tastes.

Counteroffer—A counteroffer is a statement by the offeree which has the legal effect of rejecting the offer and of proposing a new offer to the offeror.

Credit—Credit is that which is extended to the buyer or borrower on the seller or lender's belief that that which is given will be repaid.

Credit Report—A credit report refers to the document from a credit reporting agency setting forth a credit rating and pertinent financial data concerning a person or a company, which is used by banks, lenders, merchants, and suppliers in evaluating a credit risk.

Cyberspace—Cyberspace is another name for the internet.

Damages—In general, damages refers to monetary compensation which the law awards to one who has been injured by the actions of another, such as in the case of tortious conduct or breach of contractual obligations.

Default—Default is a failure to discharge a duty or do that which ought to be done.

Disclosure—Disclosure is the act of disclosing or revealing that which is secret or not fully understood. The Truth in Lending Act provides that there be disclosure to the consumer of certain information deemed basic to an intelligent assessment of a credit transaction.

Discount Rate—The discount rate is the percentage of the face amount of commercial paper which a holder pays when he transfers such paper to a financial institution for cash or credit.

Download—A download is the transfer of files or software from a remote computer to the user's computer.

Duress—Duress is action by one person which propels another person to do something he or she would not otherwise do.

E-Mail—E-mail is computer-to-computer messages between one or more individuals via the Internet.

Excuse—An excuse is a matter alleged as a reason for relief or exemption from some duty or obligation.

Federal Trade Commission—The Federal Trade Commission is an agency of the federal government created in 1914 for the purpose of promoting free and fair competition in interstate commerce through the prevention of general trade restraints such as price-fixing agreements, false advertising, boycotts, illegal combinations of competitors and other unfair methods of competition.

Filter—Filter is software the user can buy that lets the user block access to websites and content that they may find unsuitable.

Finance Charge—A finance charge is any charge assessed for an extension of credit, including interest.

Fraud—Fraud is a false representation of a matter of fact, whether by words or by conduct, by false or misleading allegations, or by concealment of that which should have been disclosed, which deceives and is intended to deceive another so that he shall act upon it to his legal injury.

Free on Board (FOB)—Free on board is a commercial term that signifies a contractual agreement between a buyer and a seller to have the subject of a sale delivered to a designated place, usually either the place of shipment or the place of destination, without expense to the buyer.

Frustration of Purpose—Frustration of purpose in contract law occurs when an implied condition of an agreement does not occur or ceases to exist without fault of either party such that the absence of the implied condition frustrates one party intentions in making the agreement.

General Damages—General damages are those damages directly referable to the breach or tortious act and which can be readily proven to have been sustained and for which the injured party should be compensated as a matter of right. Also referred to as actual or compensatory damages.

Grace Period—The grace period is the period beyond the due date set forth in the contract during which time payment may be made without incurring a penalty.

Impossibility—Impossibility is a defense to breach of contract and arises when performance is impossible due to the destruction of the subject matter of the contract or the death of a person necessary for performance.

Incapacity—Incapacity is a defense to breach of contract which refers to a lack of legal, physical or intellectual power to enter into a contract.

Indemnification Clause—An indemnification clause in a contract refers to the agreement by one party to secure the other party against loss or damage which may occur in the future in connection with performance of the contract.

Installment Contract—An installment contract is one in which the obligation, such as the payment of money, is divided into a series of successive performances over a period of time.

Interest—Interest is the compensation paid for the use of money loaned.

Internet—The internet is the universal network that allows computers to talk to other computers in words, text, graphics, and sound, anywhere in the world.

ISP (Internet Service Provider)—An ISP is a service that allows the user to connect to the internet.

Joint and Several—Joint and several refers to the sharing of rights and liabilities among a group of people collectively and individually.

Judgment—A judgment is a final determination by a court of law concerning the rights of the parties to a lawsuit.

Junk E-mail—Junk e-mail is unsolicited commercial e-mail also known as "spam."

Keyword—A keyword is a word the user enters into a search engine to begin the search for specific information or websites.

Liability—Liability refers to one's obligation to do or refrain from doing something, such as the payment of a debt.

Links—Links are highlighted words on a website that allow the user to connect to other parts of the same website or to other websites.

Liquidated Damages—Liquidated damages refers to the amount stipulated by the parties to a contract representing a reasonable estimate of the damages which would result from a breach by the parties.

Listserve—Listserve is an online mailing list that allows individuals or organizations to send email to groups of people at one time.

Loan Principal—The loan principal is the amount of the debt not including interest or any other additions.

Material Breach—A material breach refers to a substantial breach of contract which excuses further performance by the innocent party and gives rise to an action for breach of contract by that party.

Merger Clause—A merger clause is a provision in a contract which states that the written terms of the agreement may not be varied by prior or oral agreements because all such agreements are said to have merged into the writing.

Mitigation of Damages—Mitigation of damages refers to the duty imposed on an injured party to exercise reasonable diligence in attempting to minimize the damages resulting from the injury.

Modem—A modem is an internal or external device that connects the computer to a phone line and, if the user wishes, to a company that can link the user to the internet.

Mutual Agreement—Mutual agreement refers to the meeting of the minds of the parties to a contract concerning the subject matter of the contract.

Novation—A novation refers to the substitution of a new party and the discharge of an original party to a contract, with the assent of all parties.

Offer—An offer is a manifestation of willingness to enter into a bargain which invites the acceptance of the person to whom the offer is made.

Offeree—An offeree is the person to whom an offer is made.

Offeror—An offeror is the person who makes an offer.

Online Service—An online service is an ISP with added information, entertainment and shopping features.

Oral Agreement—An oral agreement is one which is not in writing or not signed by the parties.

Parol Evidence Rule—The parol evidence rule is the doctrine which holds that the written terms of an agreement may not be varied by prior or oral agreements.

Password—A password is a personal code that the user selects to access their account with their ISP.

Performance—Performance refers to the completion of one's contractual obligation.

Privacy Policy—A privacy policy is a statement on a website describing what information about the user is collected by the site and how it is used.

Privity of Contract—Privity of contract refers to the relationship between the parties to a contract.

Purchase Order—A purchase order is a document which authorizes a seller to deliver goods and is considered an offer which is accepted upon delivery.

Quantum Meruit—Quantum meruit is an equitable doctrine based on unjust enrichment which refers to the extent of liability in a contract implied by law, also known as a quasi-contract, wherein the court infers a reasonable amount payable for goods and services even when there is no contract between the parties.

Quasi-Contract—Quasi contract refers to the legal obligation invoked in the absence of an agreement where there has been unjust enrichment.

Quid Pro Quo—Quid pro quo refers to the mutual consideration which passes between the parties to a contract rendering it valid and binding.

Reformation—Reformation is an equitable remedy which calls for the rewriting of a contract involving a mutual mistake or fraud.

Remedy—The remedy is the means by which a right is enforced or a violation of a right is compensated.

Repudiation—Repudiation refers to the refusal by one party to a contract to perform a duty or obligation owed to the other party.

Rescission—Rescission refers to the cancellation of a contract which returns the parties to the positions they were in before the contract was made.

Restatement of Contracts—The Restatement of Contracts is a series of volumes written and published by the American Law Institute (ALI) which attempts to state an orderly explanation of the current and evolving law of contracts, and sets forth a proposed direction which the ALI believes contract law should follow.

Restitution—Restitution refers to the act of restoring a party to a contract to their status quo, i.e., the position the party would have been in if no contract had been made.

Screen Name—A screen name is the name the user selects to be known by when the user communicates online.

Search Engine—A search engine is a function that lets the user search for information and websites. Search engines or search functions may be found on many web sites.

Specific Performance—Specific performance is the equitable remedy available to an aggrieved party where there has been a breach of contract which requires the guilty party to perform his or her obligations under the contract.

Statute of Frauds—The Statute of Frauds refers to the requirement that certain contracts must be in writing to be legally enforceable.

Substantial Performance—Substantial performance refers to the performance of all of the essential terms of a contract so that the purpose of the contract has been accomplished giving rise to the right to compensation even though minor omissions may exist.

Unconscionable—Unconscionable refers to the condition of a contract which is so one-sided and detrimental to the interest of one of the parties that it operates to render the contract unenforceable.

Uniform Commercial Code (UCC)—The UCC is a code of laws governing commercial transactions which was designed to bring uniformity to the laws of the various states.

Unilateral Contract—A unilateral contract is a contract whereby one party makes a promise to do or refrain from doing something in return for actual performance by the other party.

URL (Uniform Resource Locator)—A URL is the address that lets the user locate a particular site. For example, http://www.ftc.gov is the URL for the Federal Trade Commission. Government URLs end in .gov and non-profit organizations and trade associations end in .org. Commercial companies generally end in .com, although additional suffixes or domains may be used as the number of internet businesses grows.

Usury—Usury refers to an excessive and illegal rate of interest.

Virus—A virus is a file maliciously planted in the user's computer that can damage files and disrupt their system.

Waiver—Waiver refers to an intentional and voluntary surrender of a known right.

Website—A website is an internet destination where the user can look at and retrieve data. All the web sites in the world, linked together, make up the World Wide Web or the "Web."

BIBLIOGRAPHY

The American Express Company (Date Visited: April 2002) <http://www.americanexpress.com,>.

Black's Law Dictionary, Fifth Edition. St. Paul, MN: West Publishing Company, 1979.

Call For Action (Date Visited: April 2002) <http://www.callforaction.org>.

The Consumer Information Center (Date Visited: April 2002) <http://www.pueblo.gsa.gov>.

The Direct Marketing Association (Date Visited: April 2002) <http://www.the-dma.org>.

The Federal Trade Commission (Date Visited: April 2002) <http://www.ftc.gov>.

Greenfield, Michael M. *Consumer Law: A Guide for Those Who Represent Sellers, Lenders, and Consumers*. Boston, MA: Little, Brown and Company, 1995.

Gifis, Steven H. *Barron's Law Dictionary, Second Ed. Woodbury, NY: Barron's Educational Series, Inc., 1984.*

Sheldon, Jonathan *Unfair and Deceptive Acts and Practices*. Boston, MA: National Consumer Law Center, 1992.

Stone, Bradford *Uniform Commercial Code, Fourth Edition*. St. Paul, MN: West Publishing Co., 1995.

Zeidman, Philip F. *Legal Aspects of Buying and Selling*. Colorado Springs, CO: Shepard's/McGraw-Hill, 1993.